Angie,
Thank you so much
for supporting me in
my work, and I
wish you Love &
Light in your life.

Donna Fisher-Jackson

The Healing Path of the Romantic

Cover art: Eros and Psyche by Antonio Canova
Original sculpture in the Louvre Museum in Paris, France
Cover photograph and Author's photograph by J. Alan Jackson

Books or articles quoted or cited in the text under the usual fair allowances
are acknowledged in the Notes. The author is grateful for permission to use
more extensive quotations from the following sources:

Excerpts from *The Invisible Partner: How the Male and Female in Each of Us Affects Our Relationships*, by John A. Sanford. Copyright © 1980 by John A. Sanford. Paulist Press, Inc., New York/Mahwah, NJ. Reprinted by permission of Paulist Press, Inc. www.paulistpress.com

From *Romancing the Shadow* by Connie Zweig, Ph.D. and Steve Wolf, Ph.D., copyright © 1997 by Connie Zweig, Ph.D., and Steve Wolf, Ph.D. Used by permission of Ballantine Books, a division of Random House, Inc.

ISBN: 1-4392-5001-4
ISBN-13: 9781439250013

To order additional copies, please contact us.
BookSurge
www.booksurge.com
1-866-308-6235
orders@booksurge.com

The Healing Path of the Romantic

Type Four of the Enneagram Personality Type System

Donna M. Fisher-Jackson, M.A.

2009

Dedication

To Jim for his love and support all these years; and for weathering
the stormy seas of relationship with a Romantic.

Table of contents

Acknowledgements

My gratitude goes to my Romantic friends—several women and men who shared their stories of what it means to be a Romantic in their lives. I am deeply appreciative of the trust they placed in me to include their stories in this book under pseudo names chosen by them which are as creative as they are.

I would also like to offer special thanks to my parents, Donald and Doris, and my sisters, Doreen and Denise, and my niece, Jennifer who all read this book in its final form, and were supportive of my bringing this story out into the world.

I also thank the friends and colleagues who commented on my book, and gave me invaluable suggestions. Special thanks goes to Connie Rodriguez, Ph.D. who was especially encouraging of my birthing this book, and acted as a midwife at many times during the creative process.

My heartfelt thanks especially goes to my husband, my best friend and my soul mate, Jim Jackson who has played a starring role in this healing journey with me. It is because of his enduring love and support that I am finally able to bring this story out into the world.

Preface

This book has been a work-in-process my whole life. It feels like a message that I am destined to share with others. I have a Master's degree in Counseling Psychology, and I have taken several Enneagram workshops, and read many Enneagram books. My main qualification for writing this book is that I am an expert at being a Romantic, the Type Four of the Enneagram Personality Type System. For almost 50 years, I have lived the life of a Romantic, and in graduate school, I finally discovered my way of being through the Enneagram. Through this discovery, I want to share what I have learned with others, and help them on their own healing path.

In the middle of my Master's degree program at John F. Kennedy University, I took a workshop on the Enneagram with Sharon Berbower, psychotherapist and professor, who has studied the Enneagram for over twenty years, originally learning the system with Helen Palmer, one of the experts of the Enneagram. I had been waiting to learn more about this system which had intrigued me for several years. During my graduate school years, I had worked at East West Bookshop in Mountain View, CA, a mecca of metaphysical and spiritual books for spiritual seekers of all kinds. At the store, they had a section on the Enneagram, and I had often peeked at those books, but perhaps I wasn't quite ready to know which type I was. I was still living a life in the rosy glow of love's illusion, and I wasn't quite ready to shed some light on that subject. At the store, there were also many world-renown authors who came to present lectures and workshops on the Enneagram including Don Riso and Russ Hudson. On many of those nights, I was working at the sales desk, and absorbed the information from their books and the customers' comments. But the time was still not right.

It was July, 2002 when I took that first Enneagram workshop with Berbower at John F. Kennedy University. As I listened to the panels of people with different personality types, I was intrigued by their personal stories, but I didn't feel a strong connection. When I heard Berbower speak of the Type Four, The Romantic, it went right through me like an arrow. While some students were unsure of which type they resonated most with, I knew beyond a shadow of a doubt. I knew that I was living the life of a Romantic. It was like a thousand light bulbs turned on lighting up all the way back to my childhood. For the first time, I had an understanding of why I had felt this longing all my life, and had lived with these illusions of love relationships. The Enneagram shed light on behavioral patterns that I had been expressing most of my life.

I know a lot of people shy away from being typecast or labeled, but for me, it was a liberating experience. I knew that it wasn't an end in itself that I was more than just the type, and it was more like a starting point where I could grow and evolve within the type. The insight helped me to see relationship patterns that I had been living with for years, and freed me to finally let go of those illusions around love. I began to see a different way of being in relationship that could lead to a healthier, more mature love. Even though I had been married at that time for 18 years, I was still living my life longing for a more romantic, perfect relationship. And even though my husband had tried to do his best to live up to my image of Prince Charming, he inevitably came up short, mainly because he was human, and I had trouble accepting him as a real man. I can remember now saying to him more than once with sadness and disappointment that "I am not in love with you anymore. I still love you, but I am not in love with you." I wanted the infatuation stage of love; the fantasy, idealized image of love; and the "Being in the clouds" phase of love to last forever. And even though, this wasn't realistic, I honestly thought that I should be able to have that in a long-term relationship.

Mind you, I lived in this infatuation stage of love for the five years that I dated my husband along with the first seven years of marriage. I finally had to come down to earth. You can imagine that it was a rude awakening, and one that I had trouble accepting in my own marriage. Looking back now, I am amazed that I really thought the "being in love" would last forever. It seems that I had never read anything to contradict that. Of course, I was reading magazines, books and going to movies that gave me every indication that romantic love should last always and forever.

With this enlightening discovery, I just knew I had to write my Master's thesis on the topic, and then I knew I had to turn my thesis into a book. I had to share these keys to healing with the many other Romantics who are seeking that ideal relationship based on romantic love. I know that some won't be able to hear this message even if the book is placed in their hands, but my hope is that every Romantic who reads this book can come away with greater insight into their own lifelong patterns.

That is why I am really writing this book – to share this message with other Romantics, and help them heal, grow and evolve into having more mature and healthier love relationships in their lives.

With my discovery of the Enneagram, I also realized that I knew quite a few people who were Type Fours. We seem to be drawn to one another preferring a deeper kind of friendship, and a shared love of talking about relationships and the deeper mysteries of life. In this book, I share the personal journeys of some of these Type Four women and men – their heartbreaks, their triumphs, their darkest nights and their soulful lives. Some of them have healed their broken hearts, and made changes in their relationship choices. Some have found love with one person. Some have found happiness in a career path that has a soul purpose for them. Others have given birth to deeply, personal creative projects such as paintings, books and other masterpieces. There have also been some Romantics who have continued to follow the same relationship patterns again and again with different partners. Like a broken record, they are stuck in some deeply-rooted pattern that they can't seem to change no matter how many times they fall into the black hole of despair. This book will hopefully find its way into their hands to show them a different way of being in relationship.

Through sharing these personal stories, I hope to help other Romantics discover their own unique path to healing. I also offer suggestions and different tools of self-discovery that can help a Romantic on that healing journey. The ultimate healing though does come from within. After all, happiness is an inside job.

The healing path can be a rocky road filled with potholes, switchbacks and road blocks. I hope that if you need help on the healing journey that you will seek it out. It is not a sign of weakness to know when you need some professional help, but one of strength. As a Holistic Counselor, I have acted as a guide for many women and men on the healing path. Sometimes, we all need another person to shed light on the darkest corners of our souls in order to heal. It is not always an easy task, but with the help of a professional healer, coach, counselor, or therapist, they can be the mid-wife that helps us to navigate those dark, birth canals. I encourage you to find a guide when the going gets rough, and the woods are at their darkest. You don't have to go it alone.

In this book, there is enough information to get you started on the healing journey. The first step is awareness which helps you to become more conscious of the choices that you have made in your life. That is one of the wonderful gifts of the Enneagram. It is a dynamic system within which you can grow and evolve as a person. You are not limited by your type, but in time, you will see that all these personality qualities are within all of us. We just tend to gravitate towards one type more than the others.

My personal journey is interwoven through the stories of all these courageous women and men who followed their hearts. The names of the women and men in this book have been changed along with some of their personal details to protect their privacy. I wish you well on your own healing journey, and may you find magic, light, and ultimately, love on your life's path.

Blessings to all of you. Donna M. Fisher-Jackson

Donna M. Fisher-Jackson, M.A., CHT has been working in the counseling field since 1999. Donna has an M.A. in Counseling Psychology specializing in Holistic Studies from John F. Kennedy University of Northern California. She counsels women and men specializing in relationship issues, creativity, spirituality, vocation, career, and life's transitions. She utilizes the tools of the Enneagram Personality Type System, Hypnotherapy, Dreamwork, Jungian and Transpersonal Psychology, Western Astrology and the Mythic Tarot in her counseling work. Originally from Cape Cod, Massachusetts, Donna now lives in the Sierra Nevada foothills of Northern California with her husband, Jim of more than 25 years, and her two cats, Apollo and Zeus. Her counseling business is Iris Holistic Counseling Services at www.DonnaFisherJackson.com To receive Donna's newsletter, *Iris Insights*, and to schedule in person or phone counseling sessions, visit her website for all the details.

Introduction:
The Enneagram Personality Type System

The Enneagram Personality Type System is a modern psycho-spiritual tool which has its roots in the ancient wisdom traditions. It is this history that gives the system a lot of depth and room for different interpretations. There are many uses for the Enneagram such as personal exploration as well as to have a better understanding of family, friends, and co-workers. The system can also be used in its highest expression as a tool of evolution helping an individual tap into their true essence, living more consciously in their life and expressing more of their whole Being. (In this book, I will use the words Self and Being interchangeably to refer to the personality as a whole with its conscious and unconscious parts.) Living more in our Being or Self indicates a higher expression of oneself which is more in alignment with the soul's purpose for being born on this planet.

Various authors have different beliefs about the Enneagram system's origins. Helen Palmer, one of the well-known experts in the Enneagram field, describes the Enneagram as an ancient Sufi teaching which was brought to the west by George Ivanovich Gurdjieff, a spiritual teacher who used the early system with his students to discover their aptitudes for inner work.

Don Riso and Russ Hudson, well-known teachers and developers of the Enneagram, believe that the modern Enneagram of personality types does not come from a single source, but from many different wisdom traditions. The nine-pointed star, the Enneagram symbol (Appendix A) is ancient dating back 2,500 years or more, and Gurdjieff is known as the man who brought this symbol to the western world. Gurdjieff described the Enneagram symbol in three parts (a) a circle, a universal mandala that refers to unity, wholeness and oneness, symbolizing the idea that God is one, a teaching of the major Western religions of Judaism, Christianity and Islam; (b) the triangle, a common symbol in many religions—from Christianity with its doctrine of the Trinity of Father, Son and Holy Spirit, to the Kabbalah, an esoteric teaching of Judaism, with its teachings about the Sefirot-the spheres of God, called the Kether, Binah and Hokmah; and (c) the hexad, the symbol of what Gurdjieff called the Law of Seven, which states that nothing is static, and that everything is moving and becoming something else. When these three symbols are put together, they become the Enneagram symbol, which shows the wholeness of a thing (the circle), how its identity is the result of the interaction of three forces (the triangle), and how it evolves or changes over time (the hexad). [1]

Gurdjieff taught the Enneagram through a series of sacred dances because he believed that it was a living symbol. However, there are no indications in his writings that speak of the Enneagram of personality types. The origins of that Enneagram are more recent and come from two contemporary teachers, Oscar Ichazo and Claudia Naranjo.

Bolivian mystic Ichazo researched and synthesized the elements of the Enneagram for many years and in 1950, he discovered the connection between the ancient symbol and the personality types. The nine personality types come from an ancient tradition of remembering nine divine attributes as they are reflected in human nature. They found their way into the Christian tradition as their opposites, which became the Seven Deadly Sins of Anger, Pride, Envy, Avarice, Gluttony, Lust, and Sloth with two additional attributes, Fear and Deceit added. Common to both the Enneagram and the Seven Deadly Sins, the teachings believe that we as humans have all of these attributes in us, but one is often more dominant than the others. It is the root of our imbalance and the way we become trapped in our ego. Ichazo formulated his Enneagram system around these "ego fixations," as he called them.[2]

In 1970, psychiatrist Claudio Naranjo, who was developing his system of gestalt therapy at the Esalen Institute in Big Sur, California, went to Arica, Chile to study with Ichazo. As part of an intensive self-realization program called The Arica Training, Ichazo taught his Enneagram system. Naranjo, along with other human potential movement teachers, was captivated by this system. When he came back to California, Naranjo began to correlate the Enneagram types with the psychiatric categories that he knew, and began to expand the descriptions of the types. In his teachings, he also began to use panels of people who identified with a particular type to demonstrate the validity of the system.

Riso and Hudson also contradict Palmer, who believes that the Enneagram system was part of a Sufi oral teaching tradition.[3] Riso and Hudson write, "Naranjo's method of using panels to understand types is not an ancient oral tradition as is sometimes claimed; nor does the Enneagram of personality come from a body of knowledge that has been passed down to us from an oral source. The use of the panels began with Naranjo in the early 1970's, and is but one way of teaching and illuminating the Enneagram."[4]

Naranjo's teachings spread throughout the San Francisco Bay area as well as through Jesuit retreat houses across America where Riso, then a Jesuit seminarian, learned the early material. Riso and Hudson's contribution has been in developing the psychological basis of the types, and by connecting the Enneagram with other psychological and spiritual systems.

There are a range of names for each of the nine personality types with the most popular names being Type One: The Reformer/The Perfectionist, Type Two: The Helper/The Giver, Type Three: The Achiever/The Performer, Type Four: The Individualist/The Romantic, Type Five: The Investigator/The Observer, Type Six: The Loyalist/The Loyal Skeptic, Type Seven: The Enthusiast/The Epicure, Type Eight: The Challenger/The Protector, and Type Nine: The Peacemaker/The Mediator.

Sandra Maitri, another Enneagram teacher who studied with Naranjo in the 1970's, describes the nine personality types as the nine faces of the soul. Maitri focuses more on the psychological and the spiritual path of each ennea-type, the word that she uses, which was coined by Naranjo. Maitri believes that the Enneagram of personality is a map of how the ego or personality functions so even though we are born drawn to one Holy Idea; we each contain all nine types.[5] The nine Holy Ideas are nine different direct perceptions of reality when we are in an enlightened state without the filter of the personality. For example, when we perceive reality from the Holy Idea of Type Four, called Holy Origin, we see that true nature is the source of all manifestation including ourselves, and that we are all part of a universal Being.

The Enneagram is a self-typing system where an individual through reading a description of the types, or through taking a test with a series of questions, or through listening to panels of the different types, decides for themselves which type they resonate with. Many times, people end up with three or four different possible types, but with further self-exploration, they can then narrow it down to the type that feels the most right for them.

As I wrote in my Preface, I discovered that I was a Type Four in an Enneagram Workshop where I listened to Professor Sharon Berbower, and different panels of people representing each type. Later on, I took tests from two different books which confirmed my type. One of the books was *The Essential Enneagram: The definitive personality test and self-discovery guide* by David Daniels, M.D. and Virginia Price, Ph.D. which is a book based on Helen Palmer's typing method of reading nine different paragraphs of the different types, and deciding for yourself which one that you resonate with the most. The other book was *Discovering Your Personality Type: The essential introduction to the enneagram* by Don Richard Riso and Russ Hudson which includes their *Riso-Hudson Enneagram Type Indicator* made up of 144 paired statements which is a forced-choice test where you must choose which statement in each pair that you resonate with the most, and then you total your answers to come up with the type that is the most like you.

There are also on-line tests available on the following websites: www.enneagraminstitute.com and www.enneagramworldwide.com The different methods are all helpful tools to determining your type, and it is more a matter of preference which method appeals to you. Some people prefer the oral tradition, and like to hear different people talk about their experiences as the different types. Others enjoy the simplicity of *The Essential Enneagram* where they can just read nine different paragraphs, and determine which type they are. And then there are those who love to take personality tests, and enjoy the wide variety of statements in the *Riso-Hudson Enneagram Type Indicator* to get a better sense of their type. I highly recommend choosing the method that works best for you to get a clearer sense if you are a Romantic. Like I mentioned in the Preface, I knew almost instantly which type I was. For me, it was more of a knowing like an intuitive flash or gut instinct. For others, it may take longer to narrow it down. In any case, by the time you read the following chapter specifically on the Type Four, you may have a clearer sense of whether or not you are The Individualist/ The Romantic.

The Romantic is one of the nine personality types of the Enneagram system of personality types. Palmer uses the name, The Romantic for the Type Four.[6] Since I first learned about the Enneagram system at John F. Kennedy University through Professor Berbower who studied the Enneagram system with Palmer, I have decided to use the name of The Romantic. Some of the other names used to describe Type Fours are The Individualist, The Artist, The Tragic Romantic, The Melancholic, The Aesthete, and The Special One.

Chapter One: The Mystery of the Romantic

Unlocking the mystery of the Romantic requires a deeper exploration. As you read through these early chapters, you will get a sense of what being a Romantic is all about. What are they seeking? It may be: to be understood by others, to find a soul mate for life, to accept their true Self or to find a higher purpose to life. These are all possible life quests for the Romantic. A passion for life dwells deep within them. It is the longing that helps them to tap into that passion, and to create from a deep, soulful place. They are driven by a desire that others may not understand, but they don't often care what others think. They are not looking for approval from others, but take pride in being an individual. To others, they may be mysterious, alluring, and aloof at times, but their presence draws others to them especially lovers who are looking for a soul mate. These lovers can see their ideal image of the perfect man or woman in the Romantic. Of course, that image is being reflected back to them, and Romantics are very good at being mirrors for what a lover is seeking most.

Among the Greek Goddesses, they most often resonate with Aphrodite, the Goddess of Love, and/or Persephone, the Goddess of the Underworld. They may embody some aspects of the other Greek Goddesses, but they definitely seem to major in the ways of love like Aphrodite. And like Persephone, who is also known as the Mystic and Medium, they can delve deep into the unconscious world tapping into their intuition. They can experience all the depths of emotion from the heights of passion to the crashing thunder of heartbreak. For them, the intense feelings give them a sense of being fully alive. The deep emotions are what life is all about for them.

They are the lovers who write passionate love letters, and who push and pull back in relationships to create the intense reunions of the two lovers who have been apart. They literally bring the art of love to a fine and revered state of being. In another life, they would have enjoyed courtly love as the Knight worshiping the Lady from afar. They daydream of the past including the days gone by with former lovers and friends, and long for places where they once lived which are brought back to life in their memory. They are deeply nostalgic and sentimental about the past remembering that first kiss, that lingering touch and that soulful gaze. They save all their old love letters, and do tie them up with a satin ribbon. They keep those faded photographs, and treasure those favorite love songs that remind them of a lover. They can hold onto the past for decades locking the memories away in the recesses of their minds, or literally in a secret box kept hidden away.

Romantics may have several lovers over a lifetime, or only a chosen few, but each person they have ever fallen in love with is imprinted on their mind forever, and even when they no longer see the lover, or live miles away from them, they never forget them… ever. They are hopeless romantics caught up in the fantasy of love including all those special dates indulging in fine wines, gourmet food, and romantic settings. They love the courtship period of love, and will often extend it for the pure pleasure that it creates for them. They like to take their time with love – not rushing too headlong into love, but savoring the small moments leading up to that first embrace. The stolen glances, the accidental brushes of the bare flesh, the hidden smiles, the thoughtful gestures and the words of affection are all part of their poetry of love. Others may rush through those moments, but a Romantic drinks them in enjoying each unique nuance and subtle gesture of a lover. Romantics were born for love relationships, and even though they will have jobs, hobbies, family and friends, they will often enjoy most the art of love. They are happiest when they are pursuing a partner, being pursued by a lover, or deeply involved in a love relationship. They can often be with one partner, and dream of another all part of that mysterious longing that they cling to. Like the capricious

Goddess, Aphrodite, love is their main desire, and they can break through conventional relationships to pursue the current love of their life. They are more faithful to their heart at times rather than to a partner. If they do choose to remain single, they often pour that longing and intensity into their work, and creative projects.

The myth of Helen of Troy captures the Romantic woman. Helen was a mysterious and hypnotic woman who embodied the feminine world of feelings containing a power which was magical and magnetic. They say that she was an image of alluring feminine beauty, but I believe that it was something deeper than that. She had the ability to be a mirror for men showing them their secret, unconscious fantasies of the perfect woman. She could appear one moment to be virginal and the next, a harlot because she was a mystery of paradoxes. She could be a catalyst for a man to bring up his deep feelings which have been hidden in the unconscious.

In the Greek myth, Helen was the daughter of Zeus, Father of the Greek Gods, and Leda, a mortal woman, and when it was time for her to marry, she was approached by many suitors, but she chose to marry Menelaus who became the King of Sparta. At that time, most women's future husbands were chosen by their father and brothers, but not Helen- she chose her own. Another quality that feels connected to the Romantic is a woman who can make her own decisions, and follow her own desires. But Helen's marriage was doomed to failure because Aphrodite, the Goddess of Love, promised Paris, the Trojan Prince, the most beautiful woman in the world if he awarded Aphrodite the prize in a beauty contest, and that woman was Helen. In time, Paris and Helen met and fell in love, and Helen eloped with him which resulted in the Trojan War which lasted for ten years. When the Trojans were finally defeated, Menelaus went to seek out his wife, Helen whom he had sworn to kill for adultery, but when he saw her, he fell in love with her all over again, and brought her home to Sparta. Whether she remained faithful to Menelaus for the rest of her life remains a mystery. In any case, Helen was a woman who followed her heart, and was a lot like Aphrodite in that way. Romantics are also known for following their heart, and for being swept up by love's illusion.

Donna M. Fisher-Jackson, M.A.

The Romantic goes by many different names. They have also been called The Artist, The Tragic Romantic, The Melancholic, The Aesthete, The Victim, The Individualist and The Special One.

Helen Palmer lists the preoccupations of the Romantic, which include:

- The sense of something missing from life. Others have what I am missing.
- An attraction to the distant and the unavailable. Idealization of the absent lover.
- Mood, manners, luxury and good taste are external supports to bolster self esteem.
- An attachment to the mood of melancholy. Depth of feeling as a goal rather than mere happiness.
- Impatience with the "flatness of ordinary feelings." Needing to re-intensify one's feelings through loss, heightened imagination, and dramatic acts.
- The search for authenticity. The feeling that the present is not real, that the real self will emerge in the future, through an experience of being deeply loved.
- An affinity with what is real and intense in life, such as birth, sex, abandonment, death, and cataclysmic happenings.
- A push-pull of attention. Focus alternates between the negative features of what one has and the positive features of what is distant and hard to get.[1]

Don Riso and Russ Hudson describe the Enneagram Personality Type Four as the sensitive, withdrawn type who is expressive, dramatic, self-absorbed and temperamental.[2] They also name this type, The Individualist, because the person maintains their identity by seeing themselves as different from others. They often see themselves as uniquely talented, possessing special gifts, but also uniquely disadvantaged or flawed in some way. More than other types, they are focused on their personal differences and deficiencies. They typically have problems with a negative self-image and low self-esteem.

Sandra Maitri calls the Type Four, the ennea-type of Ego-Melancholy. She writes,

> Fours are dramatic, emotive, romantic, and seem to suffer more than the other types. There is often a quality about Fours, arising from an inner hopelessness about ever being truly content. It is as though they are eternally pining for a lost connection that has been missing as long as they have been alive…Fours want to be seen as unique, original, aesthetic, and creative…They value their refined taste and sensitivity, which they usually feel is deeper and more profound than that of others. While they often seem superior and standoffish, inwardly they feel socially insecure, afraid of not being loved and included. They tend to feel alone and abandoned, estranged and not really reachable by others.[3]

For a Romantic, there is a loss of contact with their Being. (In this book, I will use the words Self and Being interchangeably to refer to the personality as a whole with its conscious and unconscious parts.) They experience this loss as being abandoned by their mother or primary caretaker, but it really is a loss of contact with their own Being. They feel that something is missing in them, and there is a great longing to reconnect with what has been lost. This sense of abandonment and longing is central to the psychology of a Romantic. It can be so central that a Romantic's whole sense of Self is constructed around it where the longing becomes more important than the getting, and people that offer constancy and relatedness are often unconsciously rejected by the Romantic.[4]

The Type Four, the Romantic, also has two wings in the Enneagram system, which further individualizes the type. The wings, in the language of the Enneagram, are the two points that are on either side of a type. Each wing is considered a subtype of the main type. For the Type Four, the wings are Type Three, the Performer/the Achiever and Type Five, the Observer/the Investigator. There are different beliefs about the wings. The theory originally presented by Claudia Naranjo stated that each main type was a mid-point between its wings, which meant that it was a blending of the points. Riso and Hudson believe that each type identifies more strongly with one of the wings, and created subtypes based on these dominant wings. For a Type Four with a Three wing, Riso and Hudson call them the Aristocrat, and a Type Four with a Five wing is known as the Bohemian. (See Appendix B).

Riso and Hudson see these subtypes as a unique blending of the two energies of the two different types, and another way to understand how a person expresses their personality type in their daily life. They also describe a healthy expression of the sub-type, and an average version. A healthy Aristocrat can combine creativity and ambition in their life, and be able to set goals for themselves for self-improvement and personal achievement. They are also more sociable than the Bohemian subtype, and seek ac-knowledgement and recognition from others. They feel a need to communicate and express themselves to others, and create with an audience in mind. The average Aristocrat is more self-conscious, and has issues around their self-worth that can limit their free ex-pression of themselves. They want recognition for their efforts so they may focus more on self-presentation and the proper way to do things. They are drawn to refinement, culture and sophistication, and may see themselves as high class, and overly concerned with social acceptance. They may also be competitive, and look down upon others leaning towards feelings of grandiosity and narcis-sism.[5]

The healthy Bohemian, the Type Four with a Five wing, can be very creative combining their emotions and introspection with a keen perception and originality in a healthy expression. They are usually less concerned with acceptance and status, and are more personal and unique in their self-expression. They create more for their own personal satisfaction than for an audience. They enjoy the creative process more than the recognition for their creative work. For better or for worse, they are often more defiant of con-vention and authority. The average Bohemian is usually more in-troverted and socially withdrawn than the Aristocrat. They dwell more in their imagination, and are drawn to the exotic, the mysterious, and the eccentric. Their lifestyle is more minimalist, and they can be very private, seeing themselves as rebellious outsiders. They can be brilliant and intuitive, but may have trouble sustaining their creative efforts in the real world. [6]

Jessamyn, a Romantic, was an interesting blend of the two subtypes of the Aristocrat and the Bohemian. Married to a wealthy man, she did lead the life of an aristocrat being very comfortable with beautiful surroundings, including a taste for fine wine and food, but she also was a bohemian in her appearance and eccentricities. She wore long, flowing dresses which gave her an otherworldly and ethereal quality. As a talented musician and natural mystic, she had a more unusual lifestyle, and didn't care for fame or recognition in her work. Like a bohemian, she created for herself rather than for an audience. She cared less about the opinions of others, and followed her own creative muse. She led a very private and unique life apart from others.

Like all the personality types, the Romantics have a way of coping with stress that is depicted in the Enneagram as the Direction of Disintegration. It shows how a Romantic copes when they are faced with a stressful situation, and what the unconscious motivations and behaviors are. This may be called "acting out" because these attitudes and behaviors are often unconscious and can be compulsive. In a stressful and uncertain situation, a Romantic may act out feelings that have been repressed. The acting out gives them temporary relief, and postpones dealing with a problem until a later time. When a Romantic is under stress for a long period of time, they may appear to be more like another type, and may have trouble figuring out what their basic type is.

Since Romantics can often lose themselves in romantic fantasies, and withdraw from people both for attention and to protect their feelings, they may overcompensate for these behaviors by taking on aspects of the Enneagram Personality Type Two, the Giver/the Helper. This especially shows up in relationships where the Romantics swing from being aloof to being clingy. Like an average Giver, they may become overly concerned with their relationships, and seek ways to get closer to the people they like. They want more reassurances from their partner that they are loved and appreciated. Romantics may even create emotional scenes to see if others really care for them, and try to hold onto people by clinging to them. Like an average Giver, they may also conceal their own neediness by focusing on the problems of others. As they go down this path, the Romantic may need increasing emotional and financial support to continue their unrealistic lifestyle. They may feel a lot of fear at not being able to follow their dreams. To prevent the loss of this support, they may exaggerate their importance in a partner's life. They may remind that person of how much they have received from the relationship, and take steps to make their partners more dependent on them. They will create needs to fulfill, and can become very jealous and possessive of their partner.

Jessamyn often headed down this path of becoming over-giving and clingy. Married to a Type Five, the Observer/ Investigator, Jessamyn often spent many hours by herself while her brilliant husband explored his own interests through his business. After too many hours of self-absorption, she would often reach out to her elusive husband, and express her needs for attention. When he encouraged her to find a job to keep herself occupied, Jessamyn would make him more dependent on her by playing the role of the good wife by cooking his dinners, and keeping an orderly house. This would last for a few weeks, and then she would lose interest in the role of an aristocrat housewife, and go back to her bohemian ways once again. It was her need for security and her fear of having to support herself in the world that kept her in a marriage that lacked the emotional intimacy she really desired. She found this intimacy in her friendships with other women and in her long-distance love affair with another man through letters and phone calls. This other man was always just out of reach, which made him more appealing to a married Romantic. Jessamyn spent many hours longing for this distant lover.

The longing seems to be a key piece of the Romantic's personality, and they do experience the many shades of longing. The Webster Dictionary defines, **longing** as "to feel a strong desire or craving especially for something not likely to be attained." The synonyms mentioned include: **long** which "implies a wishing with one's whole heart, and often a striving to attain"; **yearn** which "suggests an eager, restless, or painful longing"; **hanker** "suggests the uneasy promptings of unsatisfied appetite or desire"; **pine** "implies a languishing or a fruitless longing for what is impossible"; and **hunger** or **thirst** "imply an insistent or impatient craving or compelling need."[7] All the words seem to capture different degrees and types of longing, but they all lead back to that deep place of yearning in a Romantic. That longing created long ago by that early wounding can last a lifetime for a Romantic. It can show up as a longing for another person, another job, another home and in a myriad of other forms, but it all leads back to keeping the Romantic from being fully present in their life. Since they can spend so much time in this longing space, they are often not here now. Where does that longing come from? How is it created in a soul? How does a child develop that longing? The roots of the longing may be revealed in the childhood of a Type Four.

Chapter Two: The Early Childhood of the Romantic

In my own experience, the discovery of being a Romantic really struck home when Berbower in her Enneagram Workshop at John F. Kennedy University described their childhood experience. Berbower mentioned that every child was born feeling a connection with the Divine, but that for a Romantic, that connection was damaged or lost altogether creating the feeling of abandonment. When Berbower described that loss of connection, I could feel the loss in my own physical body. I had always connected this loss with my Mother. Born as the second child, I have a feeling that my Mother was just overwhelmed with having two young children to care for who were under the age of three. My older sister was very self-sufficient and independent, and I have a feeling that I was more sensitive and needed more attention than my Mother could give. My Mother didn't abandon me as a child. I feel that she just wasn't able to give me what I needed so that it felt like abandonment to me. This feeling of abandonment then created my way of coping with life. From this early loss of connection, I created a set of behaviors to help me survive in the world.

Other Romantics that I have met have had similar losses as children. For Jessamyn, she was born as an unwanted child into a love relationship. Her parents were very much in love, but got pregnant by accident, and subsequently decided to get married. Her Mother left behind a budding career, and always seemed to remind Jessamyn and her sisters of what she could have been if she hadn't gotten pregnant and married so young. Jessamyn's Father was around more when she was young, but then he started his own company, and became more unavailable to his family.

Frank's childhood was less than ideal. He was born into a loveless environment with a Mother and Father who both emotionally and verbally abused him. He became a loner, and was very fearful of people especially women. He poured his energy into sports, music, movies and reading – anything to avoid spending time with his family. For Frank, his abandonment was on an emotional level which can be just as painful as a physical abandonment.

As a young child of 3 years old, Andromeda sensed the possible abandonment of her Mother. Years later, her Mother confided that she had been planning on leaving her marriage at that time, and had even thought about sneaking off to Hawaii in the middle of the night, and not telling anyone where she was going. Andromeda sensed her Mother's withdrawal of attention, and became even more clingy and enmeshed with her Mother which led to years of separation anxiety which Andromeda believes she still lives with today. Her parents did eventually divorce a year later, but Andromeda feels that this anticipated abandonment by her Mother affected her more deeply than the actual divorce.

For most Romantic women, there are also issues around the relationship with the Father. The Oedipus complex seems to be a recurrent theme for some Romantics created either by an absent Father or an overly-adoring Father. The Oedipus complex which originally comes from the Greek myth was first formulated by Freud, and it is based on the idea that a love triangle is often formed between the two parents and the child when a child is around 4 or 5 years old. The theme of the triangle is that the child is attracted to the opposite sex parent, and can become jealous of the same sex parent, and wish that they were out of the picture altogether. In most cases, the child begins to identify with the same sex parent, and the triangular relationship is resolved. For the child with an absent parent, or an overly-adoring opposite sex parent, the triangle may not be resolved as a child, and the child may then continue to create love triangles as an adult to work out these same childhood issues.

For Adia, she adored her Father, and wanted to be just like him. She didn't feel jealously for her Mother, but more disdain, and rejecting of her Mother. Adia continued to feel this way towards her parents, and went into adulthood without resolving the

Oedipus complex. This greatly affected her romantic relationships as an adult especially when she found herself involved in a love triangle with two men still trying to resolve that old issue with her parents.

Alexandra's Father left her family when she was just approaching puberty. His departure turned her family life upside down, and it never returned to a "normal" life again. In her case, an absent Father left her seeking her Self through love relationships, and wanting the attention and affection of other men. This resulted in an early marriage, but she also met another man who became a friend to her. They didn't have a physical love relationship, but it was a higher love. Even though, she only knew him for a little over a year, the memory of the relationship stayed with her for many years. Like the absent Father, the other man became the absent lover probably holding greater appeal for Alexandra than her own husband did.

In the case of Andromeda, her parents were divorced when she was only 4 years old. Her Father was still an involved parent, but he no longer lived with them. Andromeda remembers adoring her Father, and wanting to please him so much that she didn't want to disappoint him with her strong emotions. She mentioned that both her Mother and Father saw her as an "emotional" child, and didn't really allow her to express her true feelings. Her Dad had absolutely no tolerance for her extreme emotions, and would stifle her sadness and even her joy. He would get so angry at her for her genuine feelings that she would internalize this experience as her fault, and feel shameful. Of course, her Father was just uncomfortable with his own feelings, and couldn't bear to see them in his young daughter. Eventually, Andromeda was always adjusting her responses and emotions to his comfort level, and losing her sense of Self in the process.

Romantics also seem to be so sensitive that they are naturally intuitive. They can sense what is really going on beneath the surface, and the hidden meaning behind the spoken word. As a child, I was often able to pick up a lot of the unspoken thoughts and feelings of my parents including their unlived wishes and dreams which I took on as a young adult. In my early 20's, I found myself working in accounting for a utility company doing what my Father had always dreamed of doing. It took me a couple of years to wake up, and realize that this wasn't my dream, and that it was my Father's wish for his career.

Romantics are also highly creative as children, and need a lot of support and encouragement to explore their creative gifts. If they don't receive the support, they can easily be shut down. The rejection can often reinforce their feelings of being different from others, and again feeling misunderstood. Depending on whether or not they are extroverted which is being more social and outgoing, or introverted which is more withdrawn and private, the Romantic will deal with this rejection differently. As more of an introvert, I became painfully shy as a child, and withdrew more into my imaginary world at times acting like the young Goddess Persephone. I also focused my energies on my schoolwork since my desire to learn was very strong identifying more with the Goddess Athena, and her love of learning. These personality traits didn't make me one of the more popular children, but like most Romantics, I valued my need to be unique, and to be true to myself. Even as a young girl, I stood by my friends even when others tried to persuade me to abandon them to be part of a more popular group. I always had to remain true to myself. The more extroverted Romantics may identify more with Aphrodite, the Goddess of Love, and use their uniqueness to attract suitors, and may be more focused on their outer appearance at an earlier age.

As a young girl, my favorite book was *The Secret Garden* by Frances Hodgson Burnett. I feel that it is very telling of my experience as a child. In the book, the leading character, Mary Lennox, is orphaned as a young girl, and sent to live in England with her eccentric uncle. Lonely and sad, Mary feels so alone in the world, and in time, she discovers a secret garden which had been completely forgotten by her uncle. With some other children, she brings the garden back to life healing her and others in the process. For me, *The Secret Garden* became like a symbol for my imagination. Through books, I created imaginary worlds that I would play and live in. These places became a safe outlet for me, and a healing place where I could feel less alone. The books, toys and games that you are drawn to as a child can also give you clues to whether or not you are a Romantic. Fours are often drawn to creating imaginary worlds, and they usually love to read books especially fairy tales and other fantasy stories. They may play with other children, but they are also comfortable with their own solitary games.

A Romantic, Aurora remembers as a young girl always being around a lot of people, and always longing to be alone. Type Four children seem to need more alone time than most other children. They need unstructured time where they can explore and create their own imaginary worlds whether it is building a secret fort, or an imaginary castle.

Sandra Maitri describes the Romantic's early childhood experience as a loss of contact with Being or their true nature. This loss becomes a profound inner sense of disconnection from the Divine resulting in the fixation of this type, melancholy.[1]

"Like a boat loosed from its moorings, the inner experience of a Four is of being a separate someone who is cut off from Being and set adrift. There is a poignant inner sense of disconnection and estrangement from others, but more important from the depths within," [2] as described by Maitri.

Since the mother is often connected with the embodiment of Being, a Romantic will often experience the mother or the primary caretaker, who is the source of nurturing and survival to an infant, as detached, disengaged or absent altogether. There may have been an actual abandonment, but even if there wasn't, the Romantic with their sensitive nature can experience this disconnection, and bring this feeling of abandonment into future relationships.

The Romantic may also internalize the abandonment, and feel that it is their fault that the connection to Being was severed. They may feel that their needs and a strong desire for connection are the problem, and may feel bad, flawed or damaged in some way. They often accept being flawed as if there is nothing that they can do to change it.

Donna M. Fisher-Jackson, M.A.

It is easy to see how the Romantic's attachment style to their mother has set up a pattern in relationships in later life. Attachment theory was first developed by John Bowlby who came up with four different attachment styles for the mother/child relationship including secure attachment, anxious-avoidant, anxious-resistant and disorganized attachment.

Most Romantics don't have an experience of secure attachment to their mother where they are warmly loved and accepted for who they are – the unconditional love that only a parent can give. For Romantics, they usually either had an experience of being anxious-avoidantly attached or anxious-resistantly attached to their mother. The disorganized attachment is less common, and is associated with serious mental problems in childhood and beyond.

For the anxious-avoidant attachment, the child experiences the mother as emotionally unavailable who doesn't like "neediness" in a child, and encourages them to be independent at a young age. This child then begins to expect little physical contact with the mother, and can act unresponsive or angry to the mother's attentions. For the anxious-resistant attachment, the child experiences mother as unpredictable and chaotic since the mother is often out of sync with the baby's needs. The child can then act clingy and demanding, and often angry and anxious when separated from the mother.

Most Romantics have experienced one of these types of attachment with their primary caretaker as a child. In later life, they may play out similar attachment styles with a romantic partner. In a sense, they are re-creating this early drama in an attempt to resolve it, and to receive the unconditional love that they desired as a child. In relationships, the Romantic can find themselves drawn to distant and unavailable partners, or emotional and unpredictable partners depending on their attachment styles as a child.

The Imago theory developed by Harville Hendrix, Ph.D., and his wife, Helen LaKelly Hunt in the book, *Getting the Love You Want*, is also another way to understand how our choices in adult relationships were formed by our childhood. The Imago (im-ah'go),

16

a Latin word for image, refers to our unconscious image of love. This image of love is created by our experiences of our caretaker relationships. Though we consciously seek positive traits in romantic partners, the negative traits of our parents and/or caretakers have been unconsciously stored in our memory and can be more influential in the choice of a partner than the positive traits. We seek to heal these childhood wounds with our parents through romantic relationships. For better or for worse, we are attracted to the partner who brings us the form of love that feels familiar. To repair these childhood wounds, we can find ourselves attracted to a partner who reminds us of our parents in an attempt to complete this unfinished business of childhood. Consciously, we have no desire to punish ourselves by being attracted to a partner who like our parent withheld, smothered, neglected or controlled us. But if we can get this partner to love us, then it could feel like we are finally able to get the love and attention that we desired from our parents.[3]

Harville Hendrix also included another important component of the Imago which is connected with why we choose partners with qualities missing in ourselves. These qualities are often not missing, but just repressed in order to survive in our family. If we are shy, we may seek someone outgoing; if we are cool and calm, then we may seek out someone who is more emotional and chaotic. As Hendrix writes, "Being emotionally attached to this person…. made his or her attributes feel like a part of a larger, more fulfilled you. It was as if you had merged with the other person and become whole."[4] Through choosing a partner this way, we are trying to reclaim lost parts of ourselves.

It is this Imago which is a combination of qualities of our parents and repressed parts of our Self that we seek in a romantic partner. The below Imago exercise can give you insight into your own Imago, the unconscious image of the romantic partner that you are seeking as an adult. Take the time to create a safe and quiet place where you can reflect on your childhood memories of your caretakers. Think as if you were a child, and remember your parents as they were when you were young. Take a blank sheet of paper, and divide it into five sections marked **A, B, C, D** and **E.**

- Under **A,** list at least three negative traits of each parent or caretaker who raised you such as angry, depressed, critical, never there, cold, distant, etc.
- Under **B,** now, list three positive traits of your parents such as loving, generous, always there, nurturing, financially secure, creative, etc.
- Under **C**, after you have made a list of these traits for both parents, then reflect on what you wanted and needed most as a child. What was your heart's desire? To be understood, To be loved for whom you are, To be hugged more, etc.
- Under **D**, now recall the happiest memories of childhood. These can be with your family, with friends, in school, in outside activities, etc. Then list how you felt during these happy times such as loved, valued, smart, secure, calm, etc.
- Under **E**, finally, think back on the frustrations of childhood, not just with your family, but other childhood experiences such as getting angry, keeping to yourself, blaming yourself, fighting, taking care of yourself, etc.

After you have completed the whole exercise, go back and write in the following lines:

Beside the letter **A**, write: I am attracted to a person who is: (List the negative traits.)
Beside the letter **B**, write: and I expect him or her to be: (List the positive traits.)
Beside the letter **C**, write: so that I can get (Fill in your heart's desire.)
Beside the letter **D**, write: and feel (Fill in the feelings of your happiest memories.)

Beside the letter **E**, write: but I stop myself from getting this sometimes by (List your childhood frustrations.)

Once you have filled in these lines, read your Imago from top to bottom, and this is your image of love and relationship.

The following is an example of how it could look:

A. I am attracted to a person who is: unemotional, distant, unaffectionate, controlling, and withholding.
B. And I expect him or her to be: sensitive, caring, thoughtful and understanding.
C. So that I can get: to be understood and loved for who I really am.
D. And feel: special and safe.
E. But I stop myself from getting this sometimes by: keeping to myself, being unemotional, shutting off my needs, and taking care of myself.

These early experiences with our parents create our expectations for love and romantic relationships, an important area for the Romantic as they grow to adulthood. The Romantic's major in life could very well be love relationships, and they may spend the rest of their life exploring this area whether or not they are single or married.

Chapter Three: The Romantic in Relationships

The Romantic's primary focus in life is relationships. They long for connection with others, but lasting and satisfying relationships can seem to elude them. Others appear to have more fulfilling lives and relationships than they do, and so they experience a great deal of envy.[1]

Envy is the passion of the Romantic. The passions of the Enneagram types are the emotional habits which are activated when a person is caught up in their personality or ego structure. The passions for the nine types include anger, pride, deceit, envy, greed, fear, gluttony, lust and sloth. They can also be considered the passions of the emotional shadow where they were used to help one cope with early childhood. For a Romantic, others can seem to have the life that they were meant to live. Envy can then fuel a search for symbols of happiness like material wealth, outer recognition, a special lifestyle, or the perfect partner. The search can then be repeated over and over once the object of desire is acquired, then the inevitable disappointment sets in, and the object is rejected. The search for a new object then begins all over again. Envy can be a powerful motivation for a Romantic. When they feel despair at not having what they feel they need, they can become envious of another's happiness whether it is in their work, their lifestyle, or in the area of relationships. Having conscious awareness of one's passion can release the control that it has over their life.

Envy can also come out more strongly in the area of life where Romantics have more challenges and insecurities which can reveal their instinctual subtype. There are three instincts: self-preservation, social and sexual. The self-preservation instinct is focused on survival and material security as a path to happiness; the social instinct is about being driven to achieving a sense of belonging, or a place in community; and the sexual instinct focuses on finding happiness through an intimate relationship.

Sandra Maitri gives a clear example of how the passion of envy can be expressed by a Romantic, "As a Four, we might, for example, feel envious of what another possesses if we were a preservation type; or we might begrudge a friend who seems socially adept and accepted if we were a social type; or covet the sensual allure of another if we were a sexual type." [2]

Jessamyn had led an envious life by many standards. With her husband, she had achieved the American dream of owning a beautiful home, traveling around the world, living a lavish lifestyle, and doing as she pleased. But like most Romantics, she focused on what was missing in her life instead of on the wonderful gifts of her life. As a sexual- subtype, she missed the emotional connection in her relationship, and began a long-distance relationship with another man.

When the Romantic does meet a potential partner, there can be bliss as long as the intense love feelings last, but once these feelings subside, they often feel that there is something wrong or missing. That is why they often become involved in a rubber-band relationship pattern with a partner. When the intense love feelings subside and real intimacy may be possible, the Romantic starts to pull away or create a situation where the partner pulls away. With distance, the partner begins to look more appealing again, and the Romantic becomes re-attracted to the relationship. As Helen Palmer writes,

> Keeping intimacy at a safe distance is an art form for Fours. Not too far, not too near. Far enough to be able to selectively attend to the better features of a partner, near enough to wish for more. A safe-distance, where it is possible to maintain interest, to maintain the hope that something real will emerge with time, but without any pressure to commit to the present.[3]

Dee, a Romantic, had lived with this kind of rubber-band relationship pattern for many years. She was often drawn to a man who was always just a little unavailable, and unable to commit fully to her. The couple would have romantic times together, and enjoy each other's company, but as soon as she got to know him better, she began to notice his flaws. She would tell herself that she could live with his flaws, but then it would get to be too much, and she would begin to pull away from him. Dee would tell her partner that she needed some time and space to herself. After a few weeks, the longing would begin again, and she would miss him, and then call him to just meet and talk. One thing would lead to another, and she would find herself involved with him once again. It was that familiar push-pull pattern that was hard for her to give up. Dee kept thinking that with the next man that it would be different, and so she continues the pattern.

Riso and Hudson came up with three variants of the Type Four based on which one of the three basic instincts has been the most challenging in the person's childhood, and how it has affected their personality as an adult. These instinctual variants are based on three primary instincts that motivate human behavior: the self-preservation instinct, the social instinct and the sexual instinct. Everyone experiences all three, but one is usually more dominant in the person. The self-preservation instinct is about being focused on maintaining physical safety and comfort while the social instinct is about the desire to be liked, approved of and to feel safe with others. The sexual instinct is about a person who is on a continual search for connection and an attraction to intense experiences in love, and in other situations that give them that emotional intensity.[4] The Romantic often identifies with the sexual instinct more than any other. Riso and Hudson label this instinct for the Type Four as "Infatuation," which is exactly the stage of love that is the most captivating for the Romantic.

The Romantic can probably stay in the falling-in-love stage longer than any other type. They enjoy the highs and lows of this stage of love, and are not quick to settle down to a more stable and comfortable love. They thrive on the passionate reunions with their lovers, and enjoy the sweet feelings of longing when they are apart from them. To prolong this stage longer than the average six months to three years, they may involve themselves with the unavailable partner. As long as the partner is not fully available in some way through physical or emotional distance, the Romantic is able to stay in the intense infatuation stage of love a lot longer. Zweig and Wolf describe this longing quite well in *Romancing the Shadow*, "We long for wholeness, a greater unity that stems from meeting our Beloved, our other half. Eros, our archetypal longing, causes us to reach for that which is missing; our desire is organized around this radiant absence. And we yearn to melt into the Beloved, to find there the missing piece, and to lose ourselves in the paradise of everlasting love."[5]

For a long time, Andromeda, a Romantic, believed that the infatuation stage was what love was all about. Relationships had always been a main focus of her life. In her 20's, Andromeda would go through the courtship phase, and enjoy this romantic time, but then as soon as the infatuation wore off, she would as she called it "self-eject" from the relationship. For her, the relationship was over, and then she would be looking again for the ultimate partner. In her mind, she felt that her life would really begin once she found the perfect man, and got married. Now in her 30's, she sees relationships very differently.

Researcher and writer, Maggie Scarf calls this infatuation stage, the idealization stage of relationship, where the partners are seeing each other behind a veil of illusion. As the Romantic comes out of the clouds and is faced with the real partner, the realization can be traumatic. Scarf describes it as the recognition of the mate being different from the idealized image. Upon this discovery, the partner could then try to get their mate to conform to that cherished fantasy while the mate just wants to be accepted and loved for who he is.[6]

This is where the Romantic begins to see the partner the way they really are, and they begin to become critical of the person whom they once adored. This next stage of relationship, which Scarf labels as "disappointment and disenchantment," is a natural progression of a long-term relationship. In this stage, the person is challenged to see their partner as a person in their own right with their own needs, wishes, opinions and preferences, which can be different from their own. For a Romantic, the partner's otherness feels like a betrayal from within, which is partly true because the person is in love with the idealized image of the partner rather than the real life partner. When faced with the real partner, they often feel a painful disappointment and may abandon the relationship because they feel like they have fallen out of love with their partner. Their boredom with the real partner can be a defense against a deeper, more authentic love relationship.

Adia was an incurable romantic, and found the rapture of falling in love to be the pinnacle of a relationship for her. When she first met her husband-to-be, she immediately placed him on a pedestal, and idealized him as the perfect man. He was everything that she had been looking for in a man combining the finest qualities of her Father along with her image of the ideal man. When he began to show some qualities that did not fit her ideal image, Adia first looked away, and pretended not to see them because this piece of reality did not fit in with her image of him. She wanted to only see the best in him not all of him. The saying, "Love is blind" was definitely written for Adia, and it was a place where she could dally too long. In that first stage of love, Adia's feelings were up and down encompassing the heights of ecstasy and the moments of despair when she was parted from her lover. In the beginning, Adia and her future husband had enough time apart to keep Adia high on love, and anticipating their times together. After their honeymoon, their married life began to settle down into a routine. Adia began to feel the flatness of the relationship since they were together all the time. Without the time apart from each other, there were no more romantic reunions. Life began to feel mundane – something that is challenging for a Romantic to live with. Adia had entered the phase of disappointment and disenchantment in relationship, but she had no words for it. She just missed the romantic courtship of their early days, and had trouble settling down to a more stable and comfortable relationship. She thought something was wrong with the relationship. What was really wrong was that she was trying to prolong a relationship based on being in love which can only really endure in a fairy tale. The relationship was destined to change once it was tested by every day, married life.

Adia didn't realize that being in love forever is really a matter for the gods. When a Romantic tries to claim that eternal realm for themselves, it is destined to come down to earth at some point. As John Sanford writes:

> "To be in love with someone we do not know as a person, but are attracted to because they reflect back to us the image of the god or goddess in our souls, is, in a sense, to be in love with oneself, not with the other person. In spite of the seeming beauty of the love fantasies we may have in this state of being in love, we can, in fact, be in a thoroughly selfish state of mind. Real love begins only when one person comes to know another for who he or she really is as a human being, and begins to like and care for that human being." [7]

With a low tolerance for seeing the real person in the relationship, many a Romantic is on a path of seeking the perfect man or woman, and always leaves the relationship when the mask comes off, and the real person is revealed. A Romantic also has a strong fear of abandonment, and will often reject a person before they are rejected. After some time apart, they might want their partner back because once again it is the appeal of the distant lover that attracts them. This push-pull pattern of desire is familiar for them. Fearing discovery of their inner flaws, which don't match their own idealized self-image, a Romantic can distance themselves from having a truly intimate relationship.

Helen Palmer believes that this push-pull tendency highlights a concern with authenticity of feeling. The Romantic lives in a changing emotional state so they are always questioning the relationship and whether the love can last. They need a strong partner who is able to be an anchor for them, and weather the stormy seas of relationship with them. This partner needs to hold their ground during these push-pull phases of relating with a Four. If they are able to stay grounded, there is a possibility that trust can be built, and the relationship can deepen to another level of intimacy.[8]

Adia's partner was the grounding force for their marriage. As she began to get bored with the marriage, she began to pour herself into her career, and her social life. Adia began to pull away from her partner. He was also busy with his work so he didn't notice her retreat from the marriage. From the outside, they seemed to have a perfect marriage with a beautiful home, lots of friends and family around, and traveling around the world. But appearances are not always what they seem. Inside, Adia felt the longing and missed the love connection that she had once felt for her husband.

As she headed down the path of longing, she was swept away by the desires of Aphrodite, the Goddess of Love. Unbeknown to Adia, Aphrodite rose up in full bloom in all her splendor born of the white, foamy sea and demanded attention. As Robert Johnson describes, "She (Aphrodite) is primeval, oceanic in her feminine power. She is from the beginning of time and holds court at the bottom of the sea. In psychological terms, she reigns in the unconscious, symbolized by the waters of the sea."[9]

Aphrodite is not a Goddess who takes "No" easily for an answer. Adia had created her artistic life, and enjoyed wearing her romantic clothes, but the Goddess of Love demanded more. She wanted to be in love – the only way she knew how to feel fully alive. Unconscious to this calling from Aphrodite, Adia found herself heading down a path of seeking this romantic love. She wore her longing and desire for love for all to see, and it didn't take too long to attract a romantic suitor. Adia found herself attracted to a younger man who also seemed to notice her, and she began having an affair with him.

The married Romantic is also a prime candidate for having affairs. In an affair, they are able to maintain those intense feelings that they enjoy experiencing. There are a lot of passionate encounters, sudden breaks, intense longing, and powerful reconciliations with the pattern being repeated again and again. Regarding affairs, Richard Tuch came up with the "single woman-married man syndrome" because he began to see clients who exhibited similar symptoms and backgrounds. He identified the syndrome as a way to describe the relationship, but mentions that it is not a disorder, but more a grouping of behaviors, thoughts, feelings, beliefs, attitudes, hopes, and intentions that he observed in some clients involved in an affair. [10]

The main attraction for some single women who are attracted to a married man seems to be the fact that he is unavailable for a committed relationship. This very fact is what keeps a certain distance in the relationship, which is found to be appealing for some women. Like Romantics, these women seem to be drawn into the relationship with its intense highs as well as its equally intense lows. It is a situation of not being able to fully live with the relationship, but also not being able to live without it. In this way, the relationship does resemble an addiction, but for the partners in this syndrome, the relationship is more than just sexual satisfaction, it meets some unresolved narcissistic needs in both people.

The affair relationship also never has to be concerned with the mundane tasks of a day-to-day living situation with a partner. It is able to be held in a special, sacred place where both people come together for purely romantic reasons. This special atmosphere really appeals to the Romantic who loves to create moods by creating love nests where they can be surrounded by beautiful and sensual objects. In this setting, the Romantic gets to play out their dramatic side by playing the part of the other woman, the mistress, the seductress, and the goddess.

A married Romantic may become involved in an affair at a few different points in the marriage. It often happens when they move from the idealization phase to the disillusionment phase, and they are faced with the reality of the marriage. For a Romantic, it can feel like a betrayal when they see their partner for the first time without the veil of the illusion of being in love. The real qualities of the partner that don't fit the ideal image can be a great disappointment to them. They may act out in revenge by having an affair looking for another partner who can fulfill this inner fantasy. Another prime time for sexual acting out can be the redefinition and child-launching phase in their own marriage when the Romantic can again go through their own developmental challenges related to leaving home and developing an authentic individual self. Once again, they can be faced with these issues, and escape the marriage because they feel conflicted about how to remain in an intimate relationship while being their own separate person. It's the all too familiar time of the mid-life crisis.[11]

Adia found herself in a full-blown affair. It was with someone she worked with so she was able to see him often, and the relationship became her whole focus. The younger man was a bit of a rebel, and could also be cool and distant at times. For him, it was a casual love affair, and he was enjoying playing the field. It was his cool distance that drew Adia in, and kept her coming back for more. He was unpredictable – hot one moment, and then cool the next day when he was engrossed in his work. It was torture for Adia, but a familiar theme for a Romantic caught up in the rubber-band relationship pattern. Adia lived with this on and off again affair for a few years distracting herself from her unhappy marriage.

The attraction to the distant lover is often a key sign of a Type Four. They are attracted to the lover who pulls away at times, and doesn't give of themselves wholeheartedly. The tension of not knowing keeps the Four in a heightened state of intensity which they do seem to crave. There are those joyous highs when the lovemaking is heaven on earth, and then there are the plummets to despair when the lover is rejecting or unavailable. In these kinds of relationships, the Four has definitely given their power over to the other person.

For a married Romantic, an affair can be like an emotional distance regulator in a married relationship between the lover and the husband. Scarf writes,

> Triangles develop, as a number of systemic theorists have noted, when a problem that two people are having cannot be talked about (much less resolved); the focus of their attention needs to be diverted onto something...outside their own tense relationship. Triangling in a third party...offers a

means of deflecting or detouring, but in any case lowering the intensity of the primary conflict.[12]

An affair in itself is a symptom that the intimacy in the couple's relationship is out of balance. One partner is frightened about getting too close, or the other partner desires a deeper intimacy that is lacking in the marriage. Scarf describes intimacy as "an individual's ability to talk about who he really is, to say what he wants and needs, and to be heard by the intimate partner."[13] In many relationships, it is a fear of this kind of intimacy that leads to an affair. For if you have a secret lover, then your spouse doesn't know everything about you, and the secrecy and the time constraints of the affair also keep a certain amount of distance in the extramarital relationship, which also limits the degree of intimacy that can be achieved in that relationship. Even though a Romantic craves the intensity of a love relationship, they are also struggling with intimacy issues, which cause them to pull back and distance themselves at times from their partner.

For a Romantic who has issues with intimacy, an affair is a perfect relationship for them because it has set boundaries around it which are pretty clear. These external constraints allow a Romantic to be as open and vulnerable as they desire because when they are with their illicit partner they know that the time is limited, and that they will both be going back to their separate realities after their romantic tryst. There is no danger of one's separate space eroding because each person's autonomy is built into the love affair. When your partner is with you all the time, then a request for intimacy can come at any time, which can be very frightening for a Romantic with issues around intimacy.

With intimacy issues in her marriage, Jessamyn found a perfect solution, and became involved in a long-distance love affair with someone she knew from her past. This other man fulfilled her emotional needs, and added some romance and drama to her quiet life. Their love affair was mainly conducted through phone calls and love letters, but Jessamyn felt an emotional closeness to this man that she missed in her own marriage. The distance between them in miles kept her interested, and wanting more. For Jessamyn, she had found the ideal amount of space in a relationship where she could feel intimacy with another, but not too close so that she felt overwhelmed or engulfed by his desires. A long-term bachelor, Arthur who may also be a Type Four, had a fascination with women who he could objectify as the Madonna. He seemed to adore women from afar, and had trouble living with the real woman with her imperfections. Arthur preferred to worship them as a goddess, and perhaps to use them as a muse for his own artistic endeavors. Jessamyn, who lived far way, was a perfect candidate for this Madonna role. Spiritual, artistic and intelligent, Jessamyn had also maintained her girlish looks appearing innocent in his eyes. She was also the perfect "Hetaria," a confidante and muse, for him.

Toni Wolf, a Freudian analyst and close companion of Carl Jung, came up with the feminine types of women – one of them being the Hetaria. Wolf believes that every woman embodies all four types, but that one or more of them seems to be a primary influence on the woman's personality. Romantics may find it enlightening to discover which feminine type they most resonate with. The feminine types, according to Wolf, are two pairs of women: a pair of opposites that function within the realm of the personal, and a pair of opposites which function within the area of the non-personal. The personal types are the Mother, the nurturing caretaker who represents the collective, and Hetaira (daughter, *puella aeterna*) as the individual; and the non-personal types are the Amazon, the strong, independent woman who symbolizes the collective, and the Medium, who stands for the individual. In most cases, Fours would probably lean towards the types of the Hetaira and the Medium.

Hetaira is instinctively oriented toward the individual, and is often the *puella aeterna*, the eternal daughter or sister. The word *hetaria* was used in ancient Greece to describe a group of women who were educated to be psychological companions to men. The Hetaria is focused on, and arouses, the subjective, individual aspect in men as well as in herself. She is able to look at the shadow side, and can be more concerned with that side than the social persona. She also identifies more with the Aphrodite aspect of the feminine archetype, being more oriented to love and personal relationships rather than to social and family involvements. Being more focused on individual feelings with their ever-changing fluctuations, the Hetaira women may find it challenging to commit to permanence in relationships. Like her male counterpart, the *puer aeternus*, she may avoid any concrete commitments and lead a life of changing emotional relationships. In relationships, she is the woman that can be a confidante, a keeper of a man's secrets as well as a muse, an inspiration for his work. She enjoys being a lover, and a friend to men. She longs to be intimate with a man on all levels – mentally, physically, emotionally and spiritually. She is like the Japanese geishas who were known for their intellectual and social gifts as much as for their sensual skills. The mythological images that express this type are the love deities, hierodules and priestesses dedicated to the service of love; the seductresses, nymphs, witches and harlots who live freely on their own terms.

Jessamyn played the role of the Hetaria well with her long-distance lover. She was his confidante, muse and his goddess on a pedestal. The long-distance relationship fulfilled both of their needs for a while. As long as she lived far away, her lover could keep his idealized image of Jessamyn. The distance for Jessamyn increased her longing and desire for her lover. During the 10 years of their reunited love affair, they only actually met in person a few times, and though they had kissed, their physical love was never fully consummated. The love affair was a deep mental, emotional and soul connection which was able to remain idealized all those years. But like all love's illusions, they are eventually shattered by reality, and so was their ideal love.

The Medium type of woman is comfortable with her subjective experience of the psychic realm. Immersed more in the unconscious, she is open to the intangible, but often has challenges with the earthly reality, including the limitations and needs of people and relationships. Depending upon her ego boundaries and her own intuitive abilities, the Medium can be a source of inspiration or of confusion. At her best, she can be a powerful voice of the objective psyche, and at her worst, she may become grandiose, and lose her individuality and ability to discriminate as some professional mediums and psychics do. The Medium is a woman with mystical and spiritual gifts. She is asked to walk in both the physical and spiritual worlds which can be one of her main challenges. The mythological prophetess, witch, seeress and wise women: Sibyl and Norn, Sophia, Persephone and Hecate represent this type.[14]

This was one of Jessamyn's challenges as a Medium to balance the physical and spiritual. From an early age, she had resisted being in a physical body. She was born with an awareness of life on the other side, and found the earth plane a hard place to be. She had trouble grounding herself in her physical body, and even resisted the tasks of daily life finding them routine and boring. When Jessamyn was married, she set herself apart from the world living in a mountaintop home and working at a solitary job in a monastery. She withdrew from the mundane world to maintain her higher vision of life. Deeply spiritual, she focused on her relationship with God over relationships with most people keeping a distance between herself and others. Nowadays, she is back out in the world once again, and though she struggles with meeting her daily needs, she is once again sharing her many talents with others.

Many affairs of the heart revolve around the anima, the feminine side of a man, and the animus, the masculine side of a woman. When there is a strong sexual attraction for another, the anima and animus are almost always involved. These missing sides are often projected onto another person outside the marriage or long-term relationship because the projections don't survive the harsh light of everyday life. They seem to thrive in an affair outside the primary relationship where they can live on in a fantasy world. The married partner in the affair is often known to express that they don't feel like they are in love with their husband or wife anymore, and feel like they are in love with this other person who is in essence the keeper of their own soul. When a person is in need of a huge shift in their Self-development, they will often experience an intense falling-in-love as a catalyst for the change they are seeking within. If they can step back and take a look at this infatuation, and also look at their own marriage, there are usually signs of a deeper change going on in their psyche. The romantic projections catch our attention for a reason to take a more in-depth look within and at the present relationship to see where changes can be made. If they are unhappy with the present relationship, then they can take steps to make a change, but sometimes in that process, they discover that the change needs to come from within, and not in changing partners. In many cases, the affair is a symptom of a deeper issue. As they explore these sexual longings, they often discover that their soul is seeking to become whole. They can ask themselves questions around how this other person may represent this missing half or other side of themselves which they need to re-connect with.

In the midst of an intense love affair, it can be challenging to pull back, and really see what is going on. When the projection is very strong, it can feel like they are cutting off their right arm when they pull back because in a sense, they do have to take back the parts of their psyche that they have projected onto the other. If they can become more conscious of the projection, they can often see that it is not so much about the other person as about their own inner longing to feel united within. As long as they stay in the affair, they are not going to be able to develop this wholeness within.

The secrecy of an affair is also damaging to all parties who are involved. As John Sanford writes:

> "...in the long run the extramarital affair that is kept secret is usually unfair to the other person in the marriage, and, when it comes to light, it is found that damage has been caused by the secrecy. The one who has been unaware of the partner's involvement feels hurt and slighted, and, of course, the trust between the two people has been injured and may be difficult to rebuild. Also, a person who loves secretly tends to damage himself or herself. For one thing, it takes energy to keep a secret. Secrets are like corks that can be held under

water only by applying constant pressure. For this reason we lose some psychic energy when we keep a secret hidden.... We cannot try to find happiness and fulfillment at someone else's expense without damaging our own souls in the process."[15]

When the affair does come to light, it is a chance for the Romantic to take the higher road of the healing path. The first step on the path can be going on a journey of Self-discovery.

Chapter Four: The Discovery of Self

The healing path of Self-discovery often leads back to the original wound for a Romantic. This narcissistic wounding of not being valued for their true Self can stay with a Romantic their entire life, but they also have the choice of healing this original wound. It can be a turning point in their life to heal this early wound from childhood.

Seeking a guide such as a counselor, coach or body worker is often the first step on the healing path. Fascinated with their inner depths, Romantics are easily drawn to a path of Self-exploration. Through the safe and private world of working with a guide, they can find a deep intimacy in sharing their inner world with another. They can enjoy the relationship between a guide and themselves where there is full disclosure, and they know that their secrets are kept within those sacred walls. Working with a guide can help a Romantic unravel the mysteries of their childhood and the past, and help them to find meaning in their life's path. With the right guide, they can make peace with the wounds, and learn how to move forward in their lives. The only trap can be that the Romantic can become overly enchanted with exploring their inner life and the past, and not feel safe enough to move forward in their life. Romantics do have the tendency to be self-absorbed, and can often forget that others can share similar experiences. Wrapped up in their own worlds, they can become narrow-minded, and stuck in familiar behavior patterns. Being in a support group or taking classes with others can show a Romantic that they are not alone in their feelings. It can also help them by taking the focus off themselves, and give them the opportunity to reach out and help others.

The deepest healing comes within the realm of the heart for a Romantic. They are one of the Heart-centered types of the Enneagram as described by Helen Palmer. They are highly intuitive, sensitive and feeling oriented. As Riso and Hudson describe them, the Romantics are one of the Feeling Triad – they are faced with the dilemma of expressing their true Self. "At the deepest level, your heart qualities are the source of your identity. When your heart opens, you know who you are, and that 'who you are' has nothing to do with what people think of you and nothing to do with your past history. You have a particular quality, a flavor, something that is unique and intimately you. It is through the heart that we recognize and appreciate our true nature." [1]

For a Romantic, their heart was broken as a child, and they have often closed off their heart cutting themselves off from their true Being. This results in them not feeling loved or valued for who they really are. To compensate for this loss, they create a false self-image in order to receive love, approval, recognition and a sense of value. They pride themselves on being unique and different from others. The Romantics are often dealing with feelings of shame at not having had their essential qualities mirrored back to them as children which resulted in them having an inner sense that something was wrong with them. By becoming overly concerned with this self-image of feeling special, they are often trying to escape these deep feelings of shame.

By choosing the healing journey, a Romantic can re-discover their true Self, and learn to love and accept themselves for who they really are. The healing journey is usually not taken without a catalyst such as a broken heart, a lost job, or a life change such as a divorce, a death, or a major move. It is the pain and heartbreak of these changes that can lead them down the healing path.

For many, it is that "Dark Night of the Soul" that St. John of the Cross wrote so eloquently about that begins their healing journey. The "Dark Night of the Soul" is a time of stepping into the unknown, the abyss or the dark tunnel with no visible light. It is a rite of passage in one's life. It is a time when a Romantic can begin to let go of their old identity awakening to a greater identity. It is a natural process of life to let go of the old to make room for the new. Feelings of anxiety, depression, emptiness or chaos can all show up on this journey. It can feel like a death because the personality is dying to allow the whole Self to be expressed. It is as if they are stepping into a black void where they can't see the bottom, or the way out. It truly is a time of surrender and the chance to give birth to their whole Self. When a Romantic faces such a dark night, it is in their best interest to have a professional guide. A therapist or counselor can act as a midwife as they go through this letting go of their old way of being to be re-born and reconnect with their true Self.

I have personally been through the "Dark Night of the Soul" more than once in my life. At one point, I was burned out physically, mentally, emotionally and spiritually, and had to leave a career path that I had loved which I had allowed to take over my whole life. I remember leaving my job and stepping into a black void, and not having any words for what I was going through. My own spiritual quest for answers along with working with a counselor helped me to find a new career path. It certainly is not a time to do the inner work alone because it can be challenging to have a greater perspective of what is happening to you. A professional counselor can give you their objective insight, and help you to see the big picture of your life. It is definitely a turning point for growth, and if you can stay with the experience, you can discover a deeper meaning and purpose to your life.

In a sense, it is embodying Persephone, the Greek Goddess, who took the journey into the underworld unwillingly. Abducted by Hades, she was taken from her Mother, Demeter, and her life as an innocent young woman was changed irrevocably. Many women are abducted in this manner into the underworld through domestic violence, a traumatic event or through a depression which overtakes them. It is not a journey they would have chosen for themselves, but once, they are in the experience, there is insight to be gained. There is also inner guidance that can come from staying with the darkness. Some of our most profound lessons can come from those darkest hours.

Adia faced her darkest hour when her on and off again relationship with her young lover finally ended for good. Still married, Adia felt ashamed and marked with the capital letter, "A" for adultery like Hester Prynne in Nathaniel Hawthorn's *The Scarlett Letter*. During the whole affair, she never shared her secret love with anyone else, and just suffered in silence. Finally, she found her way into counseling, and found a place where she could share her darkest secrets. At least, it felt like a safe haven. Alone in her misery, Adia felt like no one else could understand what she had been through – another common theme for a Romantic feeling like no one could understand the depth of their own feelings. They often feel misunderstood, and judged for their aloofness which they only use for protection and to keep others at a distance. During this dark time, Adia set herself apart from others, and continued to pine for her lost love.

Other people may find it hard to believe that a person would focus all their energy on a distant, unavailable lover, but for a Romantic, it can feel like life or death, and they are caught up with the intensity of a love affair even when the lover is at a distance.

The Romantic is often drawn to the darker side of emotions. Most of them have gone through periods of depression in their lives, and some have been diagnosed with bi-polar disorders for their extreme fluctuating moods. Professional therapy is always important when the mood swings are extreme. There is often a great deal of anger under the depression. The anger is often directed towards the abandoning parent, but they cannot express this anger towards that parent so the anger is turned inward creating the depression. Under the depression, there is often a lack of self-worth, and a sense of hopelessness. The hopelessness is not so much a giving up of hope, but rather failing to get what they desire. They are still holding onto what they want, and feeling sadness about not being able to have it. The mood of melancholy can also come from this same sense of loss.

Romantics can spend a good deal of time in the place of melancholy. For them, it is not always a negative place, but a more wistful place where there is sweetness in the yearning for the lost object. The fascination with this mood is hard to describe, but most Romantics will recognize it immediately when you share the feeling with them. For Adia, she described it as a place of longing and sadness where the two are intermingled. It is like the next day after having been with your lover sharing a special and romantic time together, but now, you're not sure when you will see him again. It has sweetness to it like sipping a rich cordial that you can only sip slowly because it is so sweet, but the taste and texture can linger in your mouth long afterwards. That is the experience of melancholy. You slowly immerse yourself in the feeling, but it is more of a savoring than a gulping. For Adia, there were many moments of melancholy over her lover, but there were also moments of ecstasy that could linger in her memory for weeks. Adia experienced a mind, body and soul connection with her lover. When she finally broke up with him, she entered therapy, and began an inner journey of healing.

The Romantic often first searches for their true Self in relationships. As Connie Zweig writes in *The Holy Longing*, "So the purpose of love is not what it seems…its inner purpose is to evoke an image of the long-lost beloved, whose call initiates an unpredictable and sometimes painful journey back to the Self." [2]

Romantics have an unconscious belief that their true Self will emerge through being loved deeply and completely by a partner. When they experience this kind of love, they begin to imagine being a satisfied person who is whole and happy unto themselves without needing to yearn for something more, but the picture doesn't usually last too long because they are still looking outside themselves for what they need. It is the longing to reconnect with their Being that leads Romantics to look outside themselves for the answer, but this search only offers limited gratification because only reconnection with their own Being will satisfy their sense of lack. Their constant search for someone or something outside themselves protects them from an inner sense of deficiency. As long as they keep searching for the perfect thing that will bring them happiness then they never have to face the truth that external people, places and things are never going to fully satisfy their desires. If this truth is faced, then the inner attitude of longing would have to be given up, and some painful inner feelings would have to be faced. It is this longing that keeps the Romantic connected with the lost beloved, first experienced as the mother or primary parent, and then later with the lost lover. To let go of this longing means letting go of this beloved which leaves them feeling really lost and adrift. Thus, they remain loyal to the beloved in the hope of staying connected with Being in some convoluted way.[3]

Romantics are good at being introspective, but now they need to work through the layers peeling away the false self-image to uncover the true Self underneath. There is often a lot of real feelings to be processed before they can get to the deeper healing. The physical body stores all those unexpressed emotions until they are ready to release them. They are very good at dramatizing their feelings, and only going to emotions that are comfortable for them like the heights of joy and the depths of melancholy. They don't always have a familiarity with the full range of emotions. They are drawn to the intensity of emotions, but don't have tolerance for the more ordinary feelings. In their healing journey, they can learn how to tap into their feelings, and allow the real feelings to come up more. Expressing those real feelings creates a more authentic way of being in the world.

As they work through the layers, Romantics can begin to have a more realistic and bigger view of their childhood. Once they have felt the anger and sadness around their original wound, they can then begin to view their parents differently, and see them as human beings with their own set of strengths and weaknesses influenced by their own past. In time, they can even reach forgiveness, and find a place of freedom from the past. This can be challenging for a Romantic because they do tend to hold onto the past. They often feel nostalgic about the past even when it is filled with painful memories. Holding onto the past defines them in some way. In order to re-define themselves, they do have to let go of the self-image that they have held onto such as the lost child, the abandoned one, or the outsider. Once they can release this attachment to the past, then they are more free to move forward and to live a more authentic life.

Romantics are often confused about their identity, and it is no wonder since they base their identity on their changing feelings. Since their feelings are always changing, then their identity is always shifting. The way Romantics cope with this dilemma is to cultivate certain feelings that are acceptable, and then to reject the ones that are not acceptable or true for them. Instead of experiencing a spontaneous flow of feelings in the moment, a Romantic may dream about people and events that stir up familiar emotions that reflect who they feel they are even if the feelings are painful. Whatever these feelings are, Romantics like to intensify them to bolster their sense of Self, and to feel more alive. For example, they may play a certain kind of music that reminds them of a lost lover to trigger a certain feeling state that feels more like themselves. When Romantics go down this path of manipulating their feelings, they are spending more time living in their imagination rather than in the real world. This is how the Romantic creates an internalized self image, which Riso and Hudson label as the "Fantasy Self."[4]

This Fantasy Self is an ideal self for the Type Four. It is usually based on idealized qualities that are almost always unattainable even with hard work and discipline. The Fantasy Self is thus by its very nature out of reach, and linked with the Four's rejection of their own real qualities and talents. They may reveal some aspects of this Fantasy Self, but most of their real qualities are usually kept hidden. When Fours become deeply identified with this idealized self-image, they may resist any interference or help from others by focusing on how different they are from other people. Fours maintain this sense of identity through a continuous inner dialogue and referencing of their emotional reactions. They don't have a strong need to have the affirmation of others because a lot of their identity is tied to feeling different and misunderstood by others.

This creation of the Fantasy Self can suppress so much of the Four's true Self. These suppressed parts become part of the shadow side of a Four. The shadow side consists of traits that were hidden because they were believed to be unacceptable usually from some message that the Romantic received from another. It is often why they are triggered by certain people whether it is a positive attraction or a negative rejection. It is usually that they have seen a part of themselves in that person, but they are not quite ready to own it for themselves. For example, Jessamyn was often attracted to what she called "Renaissance Men." They were men that were multi-talented on different levels such as artistically, intellectually, spiritually, and in the material world. What she didn't recognize was that these same gifts were within herself. She first saw them outside herself because she wasn't quite ready to own them for herself.

Working with a professional counselor can be one way for a Romantic to uncover these hidden traits. Once the Romantic begins to discover them, the traits can give them a certain strength and confidence in the world. It is as if the energy that it took to hide these parts is now available for them to express these qualities in their life. Shadow work can be one of the most rewarding tasks that they can undertake. It is like playing detective, and noticing the different interests and qualities that they are drawn to or repulsed by in another. As they learn to accept these qualities, they can uncover long-lost dreams and passions. It is good to pay attention to our night-time dreams where these sides are often revealed and expressed.

It was in a dream that I uncovered a long-lost part of myself. In a night-time dream, a small mermaid with long, bright red hair literally popped out of my body. In the dream, I remember saying to the mermaid, "So that is where I stuffed you." The mermaid then became a symbol to me of the creative child that I had shut down long ago. In my early childhood, I didn't receive a lot of recognition for my creative gifts from my parents and teachers so I began to hide them one by one. After this dream, I began to uncover my child-like joy in being creative whether it was painting, dancing, or writing. Through creative activities, I was able to tap into this lost, joyful part of myself.

Accepting the ordinary moments of life can also make a difference for a Romantic. Drawn to the extraordinary, they are often known for creating drama and intense experiences in their lives all in an effort to banish the ordinary life. If they can learn to accept the ordinary and the feelings that come up instead of only seeking the extraordinary and the intense feelings that they most desire, they can then begin to open up to a full acceptance of their Self, and of life in each and every moment. If they can allow themselves to sink into the moment, they can discover the beauty and depth in even the simplest tasks like washing the dishes or reading the newspaper. It is this deep acceptance of the moment that can lead to full acceptance of their whole Self.

Claudio Naranjo believes that a common defense mechanism for a Type Four is introjection. Introjection refers to the incorporation of some of the qualities, attitudes or characteristics of a beloved into one's being.[5] In the case of the Fours, there is an incorporation of the ego ideal and the resulting superego demands, punishments and rewards of the parents. The holding onto of the superego is a way of avoiding loss of the beloved object, which is also tied to their sense of Self. Even though Fours may long for happiness, they are attached to their suffering because it maintains that connection with the lost object. Only through looking at this dynamic, getting in touch with the love for the lost object and finding insight can this painful pattern begin to dissolve. Introjection also shows up in the ways that they incorporate parts of those that they love and admire.[6]

Shame also figures greatly in the psychology of a Four. Shame is the resulting feelings of embarrassment, humiliation and disgrace that come with the feeling of being rejected, exposed or losing the respect of others.[7] Because the Four's true Self does not match their Fantasy Self, they are constantly struggling with revealing something that they feel, think or believe because it doesn't fit this perfect image. They anticipate that they will be shamed, which is really a projection of the shame that they feel internally by their superego. For many Fours, this fear of being seen as improper, inappropriate and flawed is a constant preoccupation in their relationships with others. To avoid these shameful feelings and the loss of respect in other's eyes, Fours may withdraw and become aloof and distant setting themselves apart from others. They can become reserved, revealing little about themselves and coming across to others as very controlled and private. Every move is filtered through their inner censor so they present in a very, formal and affected manner. Sandra Maitri writes, "Like the horse, the animal associated with this type, they present an image of controlled elegance, restrained power. There is obviously, little room for spontaneity in the behavior and, more important, in the inner life of a Four."[8]

In some cases, the Romantic can behave quite differently in the face of shame. They can pride themselves on being spontaneous with no self-inhibition, and behaving outrageously and rudely with little regard for proper behavior. This type of Romantic avoids experiencing the shame by living in defiance of it.

In most Romantics, they can defend against feeling this shame by taking a superior stance with others. Feeling and suffering more intensely than others can give them a sense of specialness and nobility because others just don't seem as attune to the inner depths of the soul. It is through their nostalgia, melancholy and other deep emotions that they feel connected to the state of Being. Because of this, they can stay in a place of grieving and mourning longer than most people, and hold onto the painful feelings.

Another helpful system in getting a clearer sense of Self is Riso and Hudson's Levels of Development for each Personality Type of the Enneagram.[9] They created this system as a way to observe and measure how strongly a person identified with their personality structure. In these levels, there are nine categories that range from healthy to average to unhealthy. The Levels of Development can be used by a Romantic as a way to see where they are on the continuum of growth, and in what direction they are currently moving. It is like a yardstick of mental and emotional health. Instead of feeling like there is no hope of changing, a Four can see a way to heal and evolve within their personality type.

Riso and Hudson believe that a person's personality type is more inborn, but that their level of development is more shaped by the quality of parenting and other related environmental factors like health, nutrition, education, therapy, and the availability of other resources. Each level represents an increasing layer of fear and defense that arose in childhood, and it may now be carried into adulthood through habits and unexamined belief systems. The more challenging a childhood is for a person, then the greater the fear that is instilled, and the more limited and rigid are the coping patterns in their life.

The Levels of Development for the Fours (See Appendix C) include three main ranges: healthy, average, and unhealthy, with three levels within each of those ranges. The healthy ranges (Levels 1-3) are the high-functioning aspects of the type. The average ranges (Levels 4-6) represent the normal behaviors of the type and where most people operate. The unhealthy range (Levels 7-9) shows the dysfunctional behaviors of this type. The levels can also be looked at as a continuum of freedom and awareness. In the healthy range, the Four is living more free of the constraints of their type, and are freer to be in the moment, and live more consciously.

As a Four spirals down the levels, their freedom becomes more constricted and they are so identified with the type that they are driven by the aspects of the personality. If the Romantic doesn't have a means of expressing their feelings, they can become increasingly self-absorbed and withdraw from life to explore these intense emotions. For them, the more intensely they feel, the more real they feel. The problem is that it can become challenging to maintain these feeling states if they are still interacting with others or taking care of practical needs. Their feelings and self image then become so idealized that reality cannot support them, which causes them to withdraw even more from real relationships and experiences to live in their fantasy worlds. Eventually, they will only interact with those few people who support their identities and emotional needs. As they withdraw from life, they cut themselves off from the wellspring of their feelings and creativity which comes from participating in the world.[10]

The Levels of Development are meant to show where the person is living most of the time. In any given day, a person's mood or mental state can fluctuate, but there will be a resting place where they spend most of their time. This resting place changes more slowly, usually changing due to a personal crisis or the result of long-term transformative work. The goal is to reach a healthy range where the Four feels centered and grounded, and more connected with themselves and their Being. In the healthy levels of development, a Four is able to let go of the belief that they are flawed, and are freed from too much self-absorption. They have a sense of their true Self, and are able to express their individuality through creative action. Their creativity may be highly personal, but it often has a universal connection. Their creativity is also often autobiographical where they explore their own personality history and how family, relationships and incidents from the past have affected them. By sharing this inner knowledge from their own souls, Fours are able to receive the mirroring that they have been seeking their whole life. Their inner life then becomes a way for them to connect with others instead of a source of alienation.

As Jessamyn, who was a musician, evolved, she came down from her mountaintop and began to spend more time with people. She began working as a teacher in an alternative school, and also started teaching music lessons. In this way, she was sharing her creative gifts with others. Creativity does seem to be one of the healing tools for a Romantic. It can help them to heal themselves, and help others in the process.

Chapter Five: The Creative Path of the Romantic

The area of creativity is a place where a Romantic often searches for a sense of Self. Fours are naturally creative. In touch with their deep feelings and the world of the unconscious, they often use art to express themselves, and conceal themselves at the same time. Suffering and the artist have been perennially linked throughout the ages, and Romantics have always understood this connection. Their intense emotional states bring them to the edge of their wounds. In those places, a Four can experience a sense of depth and of meaning where their suffering manifests into art. Creativity is a healthy way for a Romantic to channel all those deep feelings. Without a creative outlet, they can often get caught up in relationship dramas. Art is a way that they can transform their pain and suffering into a tangible form that they can then share with others. In sharing their art, they can also help other people to look deeper into their own lives. As Riso with Hudson writes,

> The Four is the personality type which emphasizes the subjective world of feelings, in creativity and individualism, in introversion and self-absorption...In this personality type, we see creative artists, romantic aesthetes, and withdrawn dreamers, people with powerful feelings who feel different from others...[1]

There are many Romantics who have become famous for their creative talents including artists, musicians, writers, dancers and entertainers. Some of the women and men who have been considered to be Romantics are: Sarah McClaughlin, Sting, Uma Thurman, Gwenyth Paltrow, Sylvia Plath, Joni Mitchell, Joan Baez, Bette Davis, Orson Wells, Marlon Brando, Joan Baez, John Keats, Percy Shelley, and Emily Dickinson.

Donna M. Fisher-Jackson, M.A.

Two famous Romantic artists who lived their lives in the spotlight are the writer, Anais Nin, and the painter, Frida Kahlo, both born in the early 1900's. Both women were married young, and struggled to balance being a wife with being an artist. Even though they were married, they continued to have many love affairs with both men and women seeking some perfect ideal, and also looking to heal some deep, childhood wounds. It is also interesting to note that both women didn't have children, but they did give birth to many creative projects.

Anais Nin became famous for her infamous diaries as well as her numerous love affairs. Delicate and petite, Anais led her life in a big way leaving a trail of drama and mystery in her wake. As a young girl, she left her home country of France to live in America with her mother and sister leaving her father behind. The distance from her father seemed to break her heart, and she poured out these feelings in her early diaries. This abandonment by her father who had left her mother was connected to the original wound that left Anais with a life-time of longing. Married young, she was an innocent in the ways of love. Her husband, Hugo was also naïve, and their early years of marriage were a struggle for both of them. After they moved to France, they both began to discover the pleasures of physical love. In France, Anais really began to bloom as a woman. She discovered creativity and freedom in the bohemian lifestyle of Paris in the 1920's. There, she met other writers and artists who encouraged her in her work. One of them was Henry Miller, who was an unknown writer at that time, who became involved in a passionate affair with Anais. Anais became a lover and a financial supporter of Henry during those years in Paris. It was the beginning of her dual life. With her husband, she played the role of the "good wife" of a banker, managing a home and a social life for a young professional couple. She would then slip away to meet her lover, Henry, and his bohemian friends who led colorful and dramatic lives compared to her monochromatic life in the suburbs of Paris. In Henry's arms, she found the passion and intensity that she had been missing in her marriage. Her secret diaries became her confidante for this other life. She longed to share her writing with the world, but her writing was such a personal expression of her Self. She didn't know how to publish her work without revealing her secrets. Anais would struggle with that choice for many years.

With a strong desire to fully express herself, Anais poured her creative energy into flamboyantly decorating her homes along with choosing unique clothing for herself. She also had a love of Flamenco dancing which led to her sexual awakening. Her sexuality was one of her most favorite forms of creativity. Over her lifetime, she had numerous lovers often spending months away from her husband, to be with another lover. With a deep well of creativity, Anais seemed to need all these different outlets for her creative fire.

Psychotherapy also became an intense study for Anais. She even likened it to a religion, and that psychotherapy was her religion of choice. In the early days of Freud, she became a patient of one of his students, Otto Rank. She became involved in a course of intensive psychoanalysis with Rank which included their becoming lovers. (This was long before therapists believed that having a personal relationship with a client could be emotionally damaging to the client.) Fascinated by her life, Otto was infatuated with Anais, and their relationship only ended when she moved back to America. Anais spent most of her adult life in and out of psychotherapy. She did find insight and guidance in the work, but she struggled to heal that original wound with her father. Her father came back into her life when she moved back to France as a married woman. Their relationship held a fascination for Anais. He compared the two of them as being a lot alike – something that hurt and enchanted Anais at the same time. At age 30, she had an incestuous relationship with her father. Some sources say that they had been involved when she was a young girl, and that she came to him as an adult believing that this act of love could heal that original wound that she had carried with her all those years. Instead, it was like opening Pandora's box, and Anais was haunted by this re-wounding for the rest of her life.

Her goal in life was always to be a writer, but she struggled with publishing her writing for most of her life, only becoming well-known as a writer in her later years. Like most Romantics, love relationships were a huge distraction for her, and probably kept her from really focusing on her writing. Anais also lived with a split between her ideal image and her true Self. In her diaries, she tried to come to terms with this split, but she was never able to fully heal it. Anais even hid her true Self in her published diaries by editing out the parts that didn't fit her ideal image. She continued to live a double life by having two husbands, one on each coast of the United States until the day she died. As a Romantic, she captured that pain and suffering in her writing. Her famous love affair with Henry Miller was captured in the film, *Henry and June* starring Maria de Medeiros as Anais, Fred Ward as Henry, and Uma Thurman as Henry's wife, June. The film was taken from her original, uncensored journals from late 1931 to the end of 1932 which were finally published upon her death and after the deaths of her husband, Hugo, and her former lover, Henry Miller.

Another famous Romantic is the Mexican painter, Frida Kahlo who is known for her haunting self portraits that express some of her deepest pain. Surviving a devastating accident at age 18, Frida's childhood came to a sudden end. Up until that time, she had been a spirited, outspoken young woman with already strong political views. Always on the move, a train accident literally stopped her in her tracks. After the accident, she wasn't able to go onto the university with her fellow classmates. Bedridden for months, the doctors put her through several operations to relieve some of her pain and discomfort. They never thought that she would walk again, but they must have underestimated the spirit of Frida. Having to stay on her back for months, Frida took up painting as an outlet for her energy. She was also quite an actress entertaining her friends and family that came to visit her when she wasn't able to walk. Her guests usually left laughing never fully realizing the constant pain that Frida always lived with. She kept that pain a secret, and only shared it with those closest to her. Her paintings became a way for her to express the suffering that she went through in her life. She did end up walking again, but she continued to go through serious operations at different points in her life to relieve the pain.

In spite of her physical challenges, she ended up marrying the famous muralist, Diego Rivera. An exceptional artist, Diego's art dominated their marriage. He was used to being the center of attention, and following his desires and impulses with little self-restraint. Their marriage was a tumultuous relationship with many betrayals, separations and other lovers for both of them. In spite of the many affairs, Frida's one great love remained Diego. She included him in some of her self-portraits because he was always in her thoughts even when they were apart. For Frida, tragedy and pain seemed to go hand in hand with her marriage and her art. Like many Romantics, Frida used her art to express the deep love and pain that she felt in her life. It was her way of healing all that suffering that she endured in her lifetime.

For many Romantics, art is a deep expression of their personal life. Many of them write, paint, act, or sing about their lives. For them, art is an extension of themselves. They usually select subjects for their art that are deeply connected to them in their personal lives. And like many Romantics, Frida never lost her love and longing for a man who broke her heart many times. The intensity and passion of their relationship was always there for Frida, and only increased in magnitude when they were separated by another lover. Frida also had other lovers, and it is hard to say whether she was trying to hurt Diego, or whether these other men really captured her heart. In any case, she had strong sexual desires probably connected with her deep well of creativity. Frida also longed to have a child which she never did due to the extensive injuries from her accident at age 18. Her desire for a child may have also been to bring Diego and her closer, or to give her someone that she could love unconditionally in the way she desired to love Diego. In any case, her Mexican culture also encouraged having children so for her it must have been a deep loss as a Mexican woman. She lived with the longing for a child for the rest of her life.

Many people wondered about her obsession with self-portraits. Some say that she painted herself so often to insure that she would not be forgotten. A former lover and longtime friend, Alejandro Gomez Arias suggested that Frida's self portraits were a recourse, the ultimate means to survive, to endure, to conquer death.[2] I wonder if the self portraits may have been her healing path, and her way of discovering her true Self. In any case, the self-portraits capture her strong, passionate nature. They also reveal the deep suffering that she felt living in a physical body that betrayed her so many times. They also captured her great love and sadness that she felt for Diego. In the portraits, Diego is one of the only human faces that she includes along with her pets and other special objects.

Death was also an omnipresent theme hovering in the background. She seemed to live face to face with death on many occasions in her young life. Yet, she outwitted the grim reaper in her many operations willing her Self to heal and recover. Like many Romantics, Frida lived her life in her own unique style. She often wore the colorful cultural dresses of her native Mexico in her flashy way with large pieces of jewelry, and many rings on her manicured fingers. She had a passion for color and drama which did extend to her personal life. She was often the center of attention at a party charming her guests with her stories. She was a natural actress. Frida lived her life in a larger than life way, the only way she seemed to know how. She also seemed to need to take her inner pain, and share that experience with others through her paintings. That could be one of the highest expressions of a Romantic's self-absorption and melancholy. If they can take those deep feelings and transform them into art, they can then share what they have gone through, and help others face their own inner pain. In a sense, the Romantic can become the wounded healer – the one who heals their own wounds, and in turn, can help others heal. Frida helped others heal through her paintings. She was a healer with a paintbrush. She painted to make sense of her life, and in doing so, she touched many people with her work, and continues to do so today. Her life story was also made into a movie called, *Frida* starring Salma Hayek and Alfred Molina, directed by Julie Taymor. Frida has become a legend in her own country, and her paintings continue her legacy. So as her friend, Alejandro, suggested perhaps, Frida has conquered death after all.

Creativity does seem to be the birthright of many Type Fours. In the creative act, the conflict that Romantics struggle with between their need for self-awareness, and at the same time, to move beyond too much self absorption, can often be resolved. In the creative moment, Romantics can harness their emotions without getting lost in them, and create something beautiful in which they discover themselves. In the moment of creative flow, they are the most themselves, and at the same time, the most liberated from themselves.

When Romantics turn inward in a search for Self, they can become so self-conscious that their emotional states become their dominant reality. Instead of expressing these feelings directly, they may communicate these feelings indirectly and symbolically, which is where art can become a means of expression for them.

Romantics may also get in touch with their creativity later in life. Being more sensitive, more introspective, and more creative as children, they may have experienced that their uniqueness and special gifts were not valued by their parents, teachers and peers. So over time, they submerged parts of their Self that were not accepted which often included their creative gifts. In a world that doesn't always value the artistic path, they learned how to choose more practical and secure paths that limited their growth, and where they had to often hide their creativity. Depending on the person, they may have tried to follow these acceptable paths in society, but then they discovered that parts of their Self were crying out for expression. Taking up painting, dance or music as a hobby may have satisfied those creative parts of themselves, but for some Romantics, that isn't enough, and their soul craves for more. Like taking a sip of fine wine, the soul wants to taste more of those creative juices. The creative path can help the Romantic heal those early wounds, and in some cases, it can lead to a whole new career.

Mid-life is often the time when these unexpressed parts of Self re-surface. For me, this creative part emerged in that night-time dream of a spunky mermaid that would no longer be suppressed. The mermaid then became a symbol for me of the creative child that I had suppressed long ago. Not encouraged by my parents or my teachers to follow a creative path, I followed a more traditional and secure path of studying communications and finance management in college rather than indulging in my love of English. And the suppression of my creative gifts continued into adulthood into my early career choices. In my late 20's, I finally had the chance to explore my creativity working in public relations for a performing arts center. Surrounded by so many creative performers, I felt myself blossom in that supportive atmosphere. Of course, I chose the position based on my love of the arts, and not for the money. The choice between following a traditional path vs. a creative path often revolves around money. We do have to survive in the world, and making a living is a necessity, but there are choices we can make to follow our chosen dreams and unleash our creative spirits. It may involve living a different lifestyle where we discover that we can be happier living a simpler life with less material possessions. Choosing to accept and love our creative Self can lead to a new and different way of life if we are open to the possibilities. Following a creative path can also be one of the ways to follow a healing path. Another popular healing path for Romantics is through relationships, the main focus of their lives.

Chapter Six: The Healing Path through Relationships

Romantics often begin a path of healing following a breakup in their relationships. They find themselves feeling depressed and/or anxious. The loneliness and emptiness can also be overwhelming. They may find themselves seeking out a guide like a therapist, a counselor or coach to help them sort out their love relationship, but they are usually not certain that they want to end it, or if it is over, they may still be longing for the lost lover. It is that familiar pattern of idealizing what is unavailable, and then again finding fault with their partner when they are back together.

Jessamyn's healing path began when her idealized relationship with Arthur, her lover was shattered by reality. Her fantasy of marrying him someday was destroyed when he confided in her that he had met a younger woman whom he was planning to marry. The bottom of Jessamyn's world came crashing down, and she turned into the jealous, wrathful goddess. She began to write impassioned letters to him, and make desperate phone calls trying to convince him that she was the only woman for him, and that she was ready to leave her marriage for him. But that was not what Arthur desired, it seemed he wanted to continue to keep Jessamyn as the unattainable goddess.

Frantically, Jessamyn began to escape more often into her illusionary world imagining Arthur coming to find her at the very, last minute before his wedding. She envisioned their reunion so vividly that she attracted another man who looked just like her lover into her world. This other man was also a creative person with a spiritual way of being. He was charismatic, and emotionally expressive. He won Jessamyn's heart with his poetic words and music. With his persuasion, Jessamyn left her gilded cage on the mountain top to be with this romantic rescuer. Leaving behind her secure and stable life, she went out on the road with a real-life musical troubadour. Matt, a bachelor all his life, came from a similar background as Jessamyn's husband, but had chosen a more bohemian lifestyle. A drifter, Matt moved from place to place wherever the wind seemed to blow him. He liked his rootless lifestyle, but he was very ungrounded. He didn't worry about his next meal or his next bed for that matter. He relied on the universe to provide for him, and just followed the signs. His lifestyle was very different from Jessamyn's upscale life. At first, she enjoyed the emotional connection, and the physical love-making. It was all a grand adventure. But when the money began to run out, Matt didn't seem too concerned. He was used to living out of his van, or landing at friends' homes when he needed a place to crash. Jessamyn was so sensitive, and picked up all the energy around her, and found it hard to live with so much chaos. She began to long for her secure, comfortable life that she had shared with her husband. Jessamyn also began to idealize her former life forgetting about the loneliness and lack of feeling in her marriage. Once again, the grass looked greener on the other side, and Jessamyn's familiar feelings of longing and envy were back in full force.

Like many women, Jessamyn was looking outside herself for a man to complete her instead of looking within for her own masculine side. She had a well-developed feminine side preferring the intuitive, right brain world that she lived in, but it left her lopsided. She had never really taken the time to develop her masculine side—the creative energy which can take ideas, and bring them into form.

C. G. Jung calls these sides in a man and a woman, the anima for the feminine side in a man, and the animus for the masculine side in a woman. He derived these words from the Latin, *animare* which means to enliven because to develop both these sides in ourselves can create a more whole and fully alive way of being in the world.

Looking more closely at what is considered masculine and feminine, I believe that the words aren't necessarily describing a man or a woman, but more a set of qualities that have been deemed masculine and feminine. The masculine qualities would be more linear thinking, action-oriented, more direct, and creating form from ideas. The feminine qualities would be more intuitive skills, nurturing, introspective and more emotional. In some cases, some women are going to have developed their masculine qualities more, and may be working more on getting in touch with their feminine side. And then there are some men who have a stronger set of feminine qualities including being more intuitive, sensitive and caring; and they have been working to be more assertive, more direct, and to take more action in their lives. In any case, it is often the missing side that they see in a romantic partner, and which draws them to that person. In a sense, they are seeking a part of themselves in the other person that they need to develop within.

As a woman, I was brought up more to identify with the masculine side of myself. I was named after my Father because there were no sons in my family so I became a Father's daughter. My sisters and I were raised to do activities that were considered more masculine like fishing, camping, boating, woodworking and sports. My Mother also had a well-developed masculine side so we weren't really encouraged to be feminine. As I grew up, the life of my Mother looked less appealing than the life of my Father. My Mother was a full-time homemaker, and responsible for all the household chores while my Father went off to work every day. At some point, I remember deciding that I wanted to be more like my Father going out into the working world, and less like my Mother staying home with children. As I grew up and began to date, I found myself drawn more to men who had more developed feminine sides. They were more sensitive and nurturing, and balanced my less-emotional and masculine approach to life. During my life, I also found myself leaning towards my masculine side or feminine side at different times. It was like I didn't believe that I could contain both – the masculine, and the feminine in myself and that I had to choose one or the other. At midlife, I began to realize that I could integrate both in my life, and for me, it has been a healing path to heal both sides of my Self. Since I had rejected the feminine at an early age, I had to learn how to heal and accept that part along with integrating more feminine qualities into my more masculine approach to life. Of course, it is still a process in the works, but I feel like I am more conscious now of when I am projecting these sides onto another person.

Most people in the early stages of relationship will often project these masculine and feminine sides onto their partners. Instead of recognizing these parts as belonging to themselves, they will see them outside themselves in another person, and believe that they are separate from them. This is what is called projection. Truthfully, these masculine and feminine sides are part of them, but they just haven't recognized them in themselves at this point. As they become more conscious of these sides, then they are able to truly own their own masculine and feminine sides.

When they are in the midst of a projection, they are not seeing the partner for who they really are, but seeing their ideal image of the masculine or feminine. As Jungian analyst, John Sanford of *The Invisible Partners* writes:

> These projected psychic images are the Invisible Partners in every man-woman relationship, and greatly influence the relationship, for wherever projection occurs the person who carries the projected image is either greatly overvalued or greatly undervalued. In either case, the human reality of the individual who carries a projection for us is obscured by the projected image.... Consequently, these projected images have a magnetic effect on us, and the person who carries the projection will tend to greatly attract or repel us, just as a magnet attracts or repels another metal.[1]

In her 30's, Cassandra, a professional working woman, found herself drawn to an older man. Jerry became like a mentor to her at work, and then she found herself wanting more from the relationship. Cassie as she was known to her friends hesitated at first to get involved with Jerry because he was married, but he was like a magnet to her. When he described a loveless marriage with no sex and little affection, she wanted to believe him. Cassie saw the warning signs, but she fell in love with Jerry, and began to have an affair with him. For Cassie, the projection was very strong. She saw her masculine side in him as a successful, hard-working executive. She didn't realize that this was part of herself. Jerry also fell in love with Cassie seeing his own undeveloped feminine side in her. She was Aphrodite, the goddess of love for him.

At mid-life, many men will seek out this missing feminine piece in another woman. In their marriages, they have often been the strong masculine provider, and have not shown their softer, more vulnerable side to their wife. For many men, they split women into Madonnas or Whores. The Madonna-type women are seen as pure, innocent and the good girls while the Whore-type women are viewed as sexy, seductive and the bad girls. Men want to marry the Madonna, but they want to have an affair with a Whore. They don't realize that these parts can be contained in one woman. They see their wife as the Madonna/the Mother, and they don't want to taint her image with their hidden sexual desires. In a love affair with another woman, these married men feel free to express these desires, and in doing so, they reveal a more vulnerable side of themselves.

Cassie played this role for Jerry, and she was also able to experience her Aphrodite side enjoying the physical pleasures of lovemaking, and being a confidante to him. Both Cassie and Jerry had major projections going on seeing the missing side of their Self in the other person. When the relationship did end, it was very painful for both of them because they literally felt like they were cutting off a piece of themselves. In time, Cassie began to reclaim the masculine part of herself, and heal her whole Self.

In the relationship of a Romantic, it is often the positive aspect of the anima and animus that they are projecting. When this positive feminine projection takes place by a man onto a woman, he finds her very attractive and is drawn to her seeing his own personal happiness with this woman. A woman who carries this projection for a man becomes the object of his fantasies, and he is no longer seeing the real woman, but this ideal, goddess-like image of a woman. In different degrees, this projection is a common part of falling in love with the beloved which is a favorite stage of relationship for the Romantic.[2]

When a woman projects her positive masculine side onto a man, she can overvalue the man as a hero, spiritual guide, and see him as a god among men. She is fascinated by this man, and can see him as the perfect man, and ideal lover. She seeks completion of herself through this man, and in a sense, he becomes the keeper of her soul.[3] As Sanford writes,

> A man who uses words well, who has the power with ideas and is effective in getting them across, is an ideal figure to carry such animus projections from a woman. When this happens he then becomes bigger-than-life to her, and she is quite content to be the loving moth fluttering around his flame. In this way, she misses the creative flame within herself, having displaced it onto the man.[4]

For the woman, she is giving her power away to the man. She is also not developing her own creative gifts, but living through the man's gifts. Jessamyn was a good example of this projection. She was highly creative and gifted with her music, but instead of developing and acknowledging her own gifts, she would admire and support the gifts of the men in her life. She had yet to own her own masculine side.

It is through these magnetic attractions to the beloved that the soul is seeking expression. The other person is a catalyst for the awakening of the masculine and feminine sides. If the Romantic can become conscious of the deeper meaning of this attraction for the other, they will notice that it is their own soul that needs tending to grow and bloom into wholeness. If they can take back the projection and own it for themselves, they have the chance to develop that potential within. As Sanford writes, "For a man this means that his life must include warm and meaningful human relationships, and the area of the heart, for the anima and the feminine always stands on the side of a man's heart. For a woman this means that her life must include a certain fulfillment in the area of goals, aspirations, spirit and mind."[5]

The Sacred Marriage Photograph by K. O'Leary

As Jung describes, the deepest longing is for the unity of the Self—the Sacred Marriage of the masculine and feminine within the soul that can bring wholeness. For a Romantic, they could look deeper at this longing that they often feel in relationship, and discover underneath this longing, that the real desire is for the unity of the Self. This need for individual development does not weaken an existing relationship bond, but can strengthen it especially if both partners are willing to follow their own path of individual development as well as growing together as a couple. To become conscious of these masculine and feminine parts of the soul is a huge step on the path of soul evolution. Jung refers to the encounter with the anima or animus as the "master piece" of individuation.[6]

For the man, embracing his feminine side means honoring the gifts of the unconscious which can include dreams, fantasies, his intuition, and feelings. These gifts can enrich his soul, and help him to follow his own personal path to wholeness. At first, the man may experience uncontrollable and unwelcome thoughts, but it is his anima who is trying to get his attention to bring him away from a path that is not in alignment with his soul. She is serving a higher purpose as a bridge to his unconscious, and when he can acknowledge these thoughts then he can begin to see their deeper meanings. For a man who has focused on worldly achievements, it can be a time to look within, and to spend more time on relationships with his family and friends. The soul seeks a balance with the masculine and feminine sides within.[7]

For a woman, her masculine side can be revealed in powerful fantasies, and in projections onto other men. If she is not able to own this side of herself, the animus can haunt a woman with far-fetched romantic fantasies, and she can become lost in a labyrinth of love's illusion. Her masculine side is trying to reach her through these fantasies, but she must become conscious of these fantasies to see them for what they really are – keys to the unity of her soul. The animus can be a guide for a woman to illuminate her unconscious, and to help connect her with the world of knowledge and how to think for herself. Through relationships, she can begin to see how she may have projected her masculine side onto her beloved. With more inner work, she can learn more about her masculine side, and own this side for herself, and in the process she can discover her own Being. If a woman has focused mainly on her personal life of marriage and family, then it may be time to explore more masculine goals such as developing her intellect in academic and professional pursuits. As Sanford writes,

> To achieve this union of the opposites within ourselves may very well be the task of life….Usually men need women for this to come about, and women need men. And yet, ultimately the union of the opposites does not occur between a man who plays out the masculine and a woman who plays out the feminine, but within the being of each man and each woman in whom the opposites are finally conjoined.[8]

This desire of the soul to develop a whole Self could very well be at the root of the Romantic's deepest longing. This drive for wholeness can be equated with the longing for God, the Goddess, Spirit, or whatever name that one uses to describe divinity. When the Romantic feels separate and disconnected from their own Being, it can drive them to connect with another person seeking this wholeness. But ultimately, the wholeness is found within uniting their masculine and feminine sides, and for some of them, they can even take it a step further in their spiritual connection.

As they become aware of these projections onto their romantic partners, they can then decide to take the steps to have a more mature love relationship. It takes the ability to see the divine in the partner as well as to see them as a human being. When they are able to hold both in their consciousness, they are then able to have a more authentic love relationship. The projections of the masculine and the feminine are the more divine parts of our love relationships, but they are also not the whole picture. Once they are able to see the partner as a real human being, they are then able to have a more grounded love relationship. For a Romantic, a more grounded love may feel ordinary and mundane at first, and challenging to live with on an everyday basis. It can take time for the Romantic to see the richer and more lasting rewards of a long-term relationship. Since they can be quick to leave the romantic partner when boredom and reality set in, they will need to stay with those more ordinary feelings and experiences, and discover where they may lead. That is the mystery of the relationship, and the discovery that there could be more here than meets the eye.

Donna M. Fisher-Jackson, M.A.

Eros and Psyche, original sculpture by Antonio Canova.
Photograph by J. Alan Jackson.

The Greek myth of Psyche, a mortal woman and Eros, the
God of Love is a fitting story of relationship for the Romantic. The
myth captures the many facets of relationship shedding light on
those darker and more challenging stages of a love relationship.
From the blissful stage of falling in love to the betrayal of the love
partner, the myth uncovers the riches to be found in long-term
relationships. In the myth, Psyche and Eros are not able to live in
their love cocoon forever. It is Psyche who shatters love's illusion
seeking more in the relationship. In the process, she loses the affection of Eros, and has to go on her own inner journey to find
her own personal truth. She is given four tasks by Aphrodite, the
jealous Mother-in-Law, but the tasks also serve a purpose to help
her develop her own masculine side. The tasks include the sorting

of the seeds, acquiring some golden fleece, filling the crystal flask and going down into the underworld.

The sorting of the seeds is an inward task requiring that a woman look honestly within, sift through her feelings, values and motives, and separate what is truly important. It is about trusting one's own inner voice.

The acquiring of the golden fleece is a lesson around power. It is about acquiring masculine energy without being destroyed by the power of it. Sometimes, women acquire this power indirectly enabling them to remain a compassionate person in the process. This lesson is about acquiring the amount of power that you really need.

The filling of the crystal flask is about how a woman can relate to the vastness of life. It is about having eagle vision, and being able to see life in a broader perspective, and to see the great flow of life. Robert Johnson writes, "The feminine nature is flooded with the rich vastness of possibilities in life and is drawn to all of them...But it is impossible; one cannot do or be so many things at once. Many of the possibilities open to us oppose each other and one must choose among them. Like the eagle, which has a panoramic vision, one must look at the vast river, focus on a single spot, and then dip out a single goblet of water."[9]

Johnson describes the last task of going down into the underworld as the most profound step of personal growth for women.[10] It is when a woman faces her deepest interior mystery, which only she can experience in her own way. It is a journey into the underworld, and a meeting with Persephone, the Goddess of the underworld, but one must not identify too closely with the Queen of the deep mysteries. If this happens, the woman can be lost to the spirit world, and cut off from her own humanity. It is when a woman is able to call upon her masculine side – her animus that she is able to move towards a synthesis of her spirituality and her humanness. It is this last task that can lead a woman to her whole Self integrating the masculine and the feminine.

In the Greek myth, Psyche's journey into the underworld shows her willingness to surrender and let go of her romantic illusions of love. She goes through her own "Dark Night of the Soul", and Eros realizes how much Psyche really loves him. Through her own hard work, she is transformed into a goddess. The two are then reunited as equals in a more honest love for one another. They have gone through betrayal, and have discovered in one another the authentic person, and they are now ready to forgive each other, and to make a deeper commitment to the relationship.

This can be a rich stage of relationship for a couple. The love of the couple is deepening to a new level of relationship with a more conscious union of two whole individuals coming together as a couple. It is a love which has passed through many tests, and is now built on being authentic with one another creating a feeling of permanence and purpose to the relationship. This is truly a time of discovering the gold in relationship.

This can be the ultimate goal in long-term relationships. There will always be projection in relationships, but there is a need to uncover the gold in the projections. The Romantic needs to see through the projections still relating to the person as a human being, and at the same time, honoring their grander vision which can see the god and goddess in the other. It is the union of the earthly and spiritual vision of the other person that can make an ordinary human relationship extraordinary. That can be the gold in relationship – two whole human and spiritual beings united in love for one another choosing to create a conscious relationship which involves continuing growth and evolution for both partners as individuals and as a couple. It is this marriage of human and spiritual beings that can give a Romantic a new vision of a more lasting and loving relationship. This can be the golden key leading to the healing of the Romantic through relationship.

ॐ

Chapter Seven: The Healing Path through Addictions

With the Romantic's attraction to intense experiences and deep feeling states, they often struggle with addictions. They don't seem to be able to dabble in life, but long to experience the depths of living. They can become overly focused on one aspect of their life like their relationship, and lose sense of the big picture of their life. They can only see what is missing in their life instead of all the positive experiences of their life. They also live with that original wound which can feel like an empty hole that they long to fill with someone or something. It is that need to ease the pain of that loss that can lead to addictions. Whatever the addiction, there is a basic desire behind it to mask the longing, and to feel better about themselves. The addictions seem to develop over time, and can show up in a number of areas such as work, food, exercise, alcohol, drugs and especially in the area of romance.

Because Romantics often do choose work that is a calling for them, they can become workaholics having trouble drawing the line between work and their personal life. Their work is often their cause, their passion, and then becomes their whole life. It is fine to have work that one feels passionate about, but it is also healthier to have a more balanced life. The balance seems to be a healing place where a Romantic can get a larger perspective on life.

As a former workaholic, I know how work can take over your life. I loved my work in public relations for a performing arts center, a place where creative energy was plentiful. At first, I treated it more like a job that I went to everyday, and was paid for my writing talents. Gradually, I allowed the theatre to become my whole life. I began to work all the time – days, nights and week-ends. The boundaries between my work and personal life became blurred. The theatre for me was my work, my creative outlet, my social life, my spiritual cause, and the employees became like a family to me. It is certainly a gift to love your work and the place where you work, but when the work leaves you no time for yourself and for a personal life then you are crossing over the line into workaholism. The sad part is that a lot of companies expect this kind of devotion from their employees where work always comes first before your family. Hopefully in the future, this imbalance will shift, and companies will realize that an employee needs to live a more balanced life to be a more productive employee.

Food is another area where addictions can creep in. Eating sweets and indulging in rich, gourmet foods are a specialty of Aphrodite, a Goddess that a Romantic can easily identify with. Creating a romantic meal with such delicacies is fine for a special evening. It is when Romantics begin to overindulge in sweets, caffeine, and other rich foods to change their moods that it becomes time to look at what void they are trying to fill.

A Romantic, Andromeda has struggled with compulsive eating since she hit puberty. It became a way for her to cope with life, and a habit that she learned from her family. Food gave her a sense of security in an unpredictable world. Now, she is a lot more conscious about her food choices, but when she gets stressed, she can still find herself turning to food for comfort.

If they lean towards the goddess, Artemis, they may use exercise to change their mood, and become addicted to the high they get from the endorphins of intense exercise. A general feeling of well-being from exercise is one thing, but when they find themselves unable to cope with life without their daily run, then they may have literally crossed the finish line into addiction.

During my time at the theatre, I also became an exercise-aholic to keep up with the pace of my work. I would go to a gym near my work three times a week, and get an endorphin high which would keep me going through the day and into the night. Exercise can also be a great habit to have, but when you become addicted to the high you receive from the exercise, then it's time to look at the habit. I found myself driven to exercise instead of listening to my body when I needed to give it a rest. Eventually, the high from the exercise became less and less, and I was left feeling more tired and drained after the exercise. In hindsight, I can also see that I used coffee, drinking multiple cups in a day, to keep me going along with sugar, having several cookies each night. My diet was not built around the right foods, but more of the unhealthy foods like coffee, sugar, fat and processed foods.

Other prevalent addictions for Romantics include alcohol, and illegal and prescription drugs. Romantics often use these substances to alter their moods, and to keep themselves in a state of euphoria. Of course, the downside is that they then have to use more and more of the substance to get high, and then eventually, they use it to just feel "normal." Any of these addictions need to be addressed with a professional counselor who is trained in addictions along with support groups and recovery programs. It is impossible to do any transformative healing work when there are substance abuse problems present. First, the person needs to become "sober" for a period of time where they feel more stable before they delve into any in-depth therapy. A Romantic, Frank has struggled with alcohol, marijuana, pornography and love addiction throughout his adult life. He has explored a variety of spiritual belief systems, and has spent time in self-exploration with the Enneagram. He has yet to find a spiritual path that gives him a sense of deep satisfaction, and fills the empty space that he feels inside. At this point in his life, he still uses addictions to ease the pain, but he feels like his life purpose is to renew his mind, to love and forgive himself and others, and to connect with God transcending the carnal mind for the Holy Spirit. Perhaps, the deeper healing will come once he is able to let go of his addictions.

With any addiction, the "Dark Night of the Soul" is usually faced when they hit bottom, and know that they can't go on anymore on the same path. Many people when faced with this dark emptiness will run back to their addiction, or find another addiction. It can often take many attempts to beat an addiction. Everyone's bottom is different from losing a job, facing a health crisis, or going through a divorce are just some of the events that can push us onto the road to recovery.

Donna M. Fisher-Jackson, M.A.

Romantics may also be found in the shopping malls in search of that perfect outfit that will make them feel special, or addicted to cosmetic surgery seeking that perfect, youthful look. Learning how to accept their physical body and looks can be a challenge for a Romantic, and it is almost always connected with that sense of loss around Self. Not having a strong self-worth based on their true Self, they focus on the Fantasy Self, and work on creating a persona or image that they can show the world. This still leaves them feeling a sense of emptiness so they continue the search for the perfect dress, or the perfect body through plastic surgery to feel better. These temporary fixes only leave a Romantic longing for something more.

One of the favorite drugs of choice for a Romantic is falling in love which can become one of their favorite ways to get high. Many a Romantic has gone down the path of love addiction. Love addiction can involve being addicted to being in love and/or to one love relationship. Since they are often drawn to the intense feelings of being in love, the emotional component of sex is very important to them for the whole lovemaking experience. Because of this desire for an emotional high as well as a physical high, most Romantics head down the path of love addiction rather than strictly sex addiction. In essence, the Romantic is addicted to being in love, and sex is only one component of that state of being. They can linger in the infatuation stage of love for many more weeks than most people could tolerate. Romantics will re-create this "being in love" feeling by pulling back from a partner to create that longing and desire only to be reunited with them once again. This push-pull relationship keeps them in a longer state of infatuation where they also get addicted to the high of the romantic drama. The feeling of being in love becomes a drug to them, and one that they find hard to live without. Where some people may not enjoy the extreme emotions of the infatuation stage, Romantics can live for that stage, and find it challenging, if not even impossible, to move to the next more stable stage of love. When they feel the relationship settling down and beginning to feel mundane, they

78

will often create a romantic drama to stir up the relationship, and bring back the "in love" feeling.

A Romantic, Andromeda now looks back on her past relationships, and can see that they were more about the courtship phase, and when the infatuation wore off, then she would "self-eject." There was always a lot of pushing and pulling going on either from her or from her partner, but Andromeda started to see this relationship pattern from a higher perspective, and began to make more conscious choices in relationship. Now, Andromeda is staying in a relationship past the infatuation stage, and observing her own behavior. It is not a comfortable place to be, but she can see that her partner is committed to the relationship, and is giving her the space to do her own self-exploration. It is a new way of being in relationship for her, and she is facing her fears and taking it one day at a time. She still wonders what true love is, but she does understand from her infatuation romances that there is more to love than falling in love.

Like the famous myth of the ill-fated romance of Queen Iseult the Fair and the knight, Tristan, many a Romantic has continued to drink the love potion which keeps them "in love" even when it is causing them serious harm. In the book, *We*, by Jungian analyst, Robert Johnson, he explores this famous tale of romantic love. In the myth of Iseult and Tristan, they take a love potion by mistake which was meant for King Mark of Cornwall, and his betrothed, Iseult. The potion causes the future Queen to fall in love with her knight, and he in love with her. Even after Iseult becomes the Queen, they continue to secretly meet possessed by this love they feel for one another. Eventually their love is discovered by the King, and they escape to the enchanted forest of Morois where they live on love alone for three years. In the fourth year, the intense spell of the love potion wears off, and they are faced with a crossroads. They have the chance to hear the call of reality. Queen Iseult resolves to go back to King Mark, and Tristan leaves the area of Cornwall, England, but not before making a secret pact with Iseult that he will always be true to her. Tristan then goes on a long journey, but he finds no peace or pleasure away from his beloved.

After years of traveling, he does meet a gentle and kind princess named Iseult of the White Hands. Despite her inner beauty and charm, he is not able to love her because he is still infatuated with the Queen Iseult the Fair. Eventually, he dies in battle broken in body and spirit. As Stephanie Covington and Liana Beckett write in *Leaving the Enchanted Forest*, "The irony of Tristan's story lies in his willful decision to suffer and die for an idealized, illusive notion of love, blind to the love that was available to him for the asking."[1] Caught under the spell of needing to be in love, a Romantic will often leave a stable partner for what seems to be an ideal lover. It is this illusion that leads them to believe that they will always be in love with this ideal partner, but the price can be very high. Like Tristan who turns down a more grounded love relationship for his idealized vision of love, a love addict can be caught in this same enchanted forest. It can be heart-wrenching to give up their illusion of what love should be. With an idealized image of love, no real lover will be able to live up to their lofty dreams. Projecting the god or goddess of love onto their beloved, the Romantic's real partner will always fall short when the Romantic comes down to earth, and is forced to remove her rose-colored glasses.

A married woman, Adia fell madly in love with another man. The physical attraction was immediate and hard to resist. It started out as a casual flirtation, and then became an all-consuming love affair for Adia. Her lover, Tony held back from giving his heart totally. He was drawn to her intensity, but he also felt like he could be engulfed by her emotions. He took love affairs more casually, and dated more than one woman at a time. It was one of those push-pull relationships that Romantics are drawn to like moths to a flame. Tony always kept Adia guessing. He never fully committed himself to the affair. Adia never knew how he would receive her from one day to the next. It was sweet torture for her, but a familiar theme for a Romantic. They are often drawn to the distant lover who pulls away at times, and doesn't commit wholeheartedly to the relationship. The tension of not knowing keeps them in a state of high intensity that they then begin to crave. There are those joyous heights when the affair is going well, and then there are the plummets in mood to depression when the lover is cold and pulls back. Adia began to mold herself to his mood swings trying to anticipate them, and be available to him when he was in a more loving mood. She handed over her power to him, and felt yanked around like a ball on a chain. Adia crossed the line into love addiction. It was an intense connection for her, and the separations were very painful. Her on and off again love affair with Tony lasted for months. There would be weeks when they would not be romantically involved because he was wrapped up in his work, or involved with a new woman. Eventually, the relationship fizzled out when Adia left the place where they both worked. Finally, she found her way into counseling, and began the long, uphill healing journey to recovery.

A love addict can live with those rose-colored glasses for a long time until one day when they reach for the glasses, and they find that they no longer work. They are then forced to see their partner for who they really are. Like with any addictions, a love addict has to wake up on their own, and as they begin to see more clearly, then they can begin to make changes.

Love addiction can often be seen in love affairs. When a single woman has built her life around a married lover's schedule, then she has dangerously crossed the line into love addiction. The changes can be subtle at first, but when someone puts their life on hold time and time again waiting for a phone call from a partner, then they could be leaning towards love addiction. The changes are usually gradual until their life becomes more and more narrow, and they wake up one day, and find themselves alone with little to no emotional support from family or friends, and a life that feels empty until they see their lover again. As time goes by, they can become obsessive about seeing their lover, and need more and more time with them. As the addiction becomes stronger, they can even suffer withdrawal symptoms not unlike those of substance abusers when the lover cancels a date, they can feel symptoms of anxiety and panic. Finally near the end, they need to just see their lover to feel normal, and can often suffer emotional pain and depression when they are apart. Like with all addictions, the love addict has to hit bottom which is often what happens when the married partner finally breaks up with them and goes back to their spouse leaving them alone. At this point, they definitely need to seek out a professional counselor for support. Family and friends that are still around can also be of help, but they may not have any clue of the love addict's other life having only seen a portion of their real life. Love addiction fills an empty space that is deep within, and the road to recovery can be anything, but smooth.

Cassandra, a single woman, found herself involved with a married man. She saw the warning signs, but she ended up falling in love with Jerry, and couldn't resist the charm of an older man. She found herself adapting her life to his schedule, and not making any social plans with friends in case he suddenly became available. Cassie as she was known to her friends found herself in a familiar relationship pattern for Romantics. Whether the Romantic is single or married, the attraction of the affair seems to be the same. The draw is the unavailable partner with the highly romantic meetings, and the infrequency of the meetings actually increases the intensity for a Romantic. When they do meet, the couple can create their own love nest where their focus is on one another with the feeling that they are the only two in the whole world at that moment. It is pure escapism and fantasy, but it is also a world where a Romantic longs to linger. They can daydream of the romantic times together, and await the next romantic encounter with great longing.

A love affair can stay in the infatuation stage for an eternity with some single women being involved with married men for years. In most cases, their opportunity for personal growth is stuck in a holding pattern because they never move to the next learning stage of the relationship. Cassie enjoyed the intensity and romance of the relationship for the first year, but then their relationship began to hit rocky times when she wanted more. She began to pressure her lover to leave his marriage, but he told her that he couldn't leave until his children were grown up which was still a few years away. Cassie wanted to believe him, but then she began having doubts when he took no steps for them to be together. She found herself spending too many lonely nights by herself waiting for his call. Without knowing it, Cassie had become a love addict. At age 30, she felt the desire to have a marriage and children of her own. She didn't want to still be waiting for her lover so she finally broke it off. Over several months, the two of them would be reunited, and then break up again. Finally, Cassie moved away leaving her job and her lover behind. The ending was very painful, and it took a long time for Cassie to open her heart and love again.

The healing path from love addiction can be filled with many false starts, and going backwards before moving forward again. Covington and Beckett write,

> Preserving a clear, unembellished memory of your addiction allows recovery to unfold; believing that you have fully recovered is a sure sign of trouble. You always need to remember what or who triggers your addiction, so you don't forget that you are vulnerable. To assume that your past addiction – or your addictability – has no lessons for your future is to risk repeating the past. There are no recovered addicts – only addicts who are recovering at different levels.[2]

The path to recovery is an inner journey where the addict needs to re-connect with their sense of Self. It's a time to re-examine their childhood, to re-connect with their inner child, and to heal those early wounds. As the healing progresses, the journey continues with re-evaluating their ideas about love, intimacy and commitment in relationships. It is also a time to discover for themselves their wants and needs in relationship as well as their bottom lines – what they can accept in a partner, and what they can't accept.

In many of the formal recovery programs for addictions, spirituality is also a component of the healing process. It seems to be a crucial step to healing to discover our own unique connection to Spirit. Before Alcoholics Anonymous was launched, Jung told the founders that the craving for alcohol was equivalent, on a low level, to the spiritual thirst for union with God.[3] Could this craving for addictions be connected with a deeper yearning for the spiritual? Could this yearning for the spiritual be behind the longing that a Romantic always lives with? There does seem to be some truth there for the Romantic who often lives with a deep feeling of emptiness and loss looking for someone or something to fill that empty space. When in essence, the deeper healing may come from re-connecting with their own Being, and with their own spiritual belief system.

In *The Holy Longing*, Zweig writes:

> When we meet the spiritual Other in addiction, we no longer consciously inhabit our holy longing. We become its captive. And we are pulled beneath the waves of desire, even to the point of drowning. But if we can redirect our longing towards the holy, the undertow can deliver us to the next level of awareness. And in this way addiction becomes a vehicle of evolution.[4]

Not all Romantics are going to experience serious addictions, but there have probably been times when they have ventured into the enchanted forest of love, and become lost in a fog of denial. Infatuated with a lover, they may have lost their way for a while, but when they came back down to earth, they may have woken up, and found a quick exit out of the forest never looking back. For those who have been lost in the forest, or are still enchanted with the woods, there is hope through following their own unique path to healing.

Chapter Eight: The Healing Path through Spirituality

Finding a connection with God, Goddess, Spirit or whatever name one chooses to call the divine could also be one of the keys of healing for the Romantic. In their search for God/Goddess through love relationships, they could discover their own unique spiritual connection with the divine.

Connie Zweig speaks of a higher meaning of romantic love. She references the Greek god of "desire", Eros, and how his godliness helps us to imagine human desire as a divine power. She believes that the god Eros lives in this space between what we have and what we desire as well as who we are and who we are becoming. His presence turns the object of our projection into the numinous Other who is present as well as unattainable. The root of this longing for the Other is self-transcendence toward a higher level of spirit and toward a connection with the divine. Zweig writes,

> …Eros *is* that driving force in the cosmos. Eros is the holy longing of the human for the divine, the longing of the one for the holy Other. And when it appears in the form of romantic yearning, it is ultimately a spiritual desire for greater and greater union of completion….Within or behind the person we love, we seek an object of worship, an *imago amore*, a means to connect to the divine.[1]

Could this be the higher path for the Romantic? To take this longing that they have lived with their whole life, and through a search for Self through the Other, they could then connect with their own unique spiritual path. Love relationships could become their path to conscious evolution. The *imago amore* the longing for a human beloved could be the stepping stone for them to the *imago dei,* the longing for the divine.

Donna M. Fisher-Jackson, M.A.

Some Romantics may not think of themselves as religious, or even spiritual, but with further self-exploration, they may discover the roots of a spiritual nature which has always been there. They may create their own spiritual practice incorporating different religious paths. Many of the Romantics that I have known have not followed one religious path. Most of them have studied different paths bringing the different elements together in their own spiritual belief system. Over the years, their spiritual path has evolved according to their own personal growth. Romantics have a desire for uniqueness, and often find one religious path too confining and limiting for their self-expression. Creating their own spiritual practice can be fulfilling and nurturing to them.

There is one well-known Catholic monk who created his own unique spiritual path, and who also happens to be described by Enneagram experts as being a Type Four. His name is Thomas Merton, and he could have easily been included in this book in the chapter on creativity. A prolific writer, Merton wrote more than 12 books in his lifetime along with numerous articles and essays, all while he led the life of a monk in the Gethsemani Abbey of Kentucky. At only age 33, his famous autobiography entitled *The Seven Storey Mountain* brought him early fame. During the next 20 years, he continued to write about his own spiritual path in his subsequent books, and journals. His books and journals capture the personal process of a Type Four. An avid journal writer like most Fours, he kept a journal his entire adult life.

Even though he was a monk, and didn't lead a worldly life, you can see in his writing the characteristics of a Four. In his life, he had a flair for drama, and even discovered romance late in his life when he met his soul mate in Margie, a young student nurse. The romantic affair which was never consummated because of Merton's vows was truly a soul connection. In his journals, Merton speaks of knowing instantly that this woman was special, and he felt he was "in love" with her only a week after their first meeting. Their romance only lasted about three months until it was brought to the attention of the Abbot of Gethsemani. Merton then came forward, and admitted his relationship with Margie, and ended it soon after. In his journals, you can see how challenging it was for him to cut off contact with Margie. In his writing, you can feel his heartbreak, and his despair of not being able to see her ever again. Surprisingly, he shares the story with some close friends, and even some acquaintances, but by this time, Merton was leading the life of a monk with more freedom. At the end of his life, he had finally won the right to live alone in his hermitage though he does complain of the constant visitations from others. At that same time, Merton often went on trips to speak about his contemplative life so he really didn't get to spend as much time in silence and solitude as he wished.

In Jungian terms, the relationship with Margie was a key step in his path to individuation. In meeting her, Merton came to terms with his own anima, the feminine side of himself. In embracing this part, he embraced the wholeness of his Self. In loving this woman, he healed a deep wound with the first woman of his life, his Mother. The relationship with his Mother had been distant and critical, and when she died, Merton was only 6 years old. Feeling rejected and abandoned by his Mother, it seems that Merton needed a physical woman to love and accept him so that he could fully love and accept his whole Self. It is interesting to note that Merton attracted this relationship into his life to complete his quest for the feminine. In his journals, he even noted that he saw this as a final and necessary step to becoming a contemplative master. Because of this brief relationship, Merton's life came full circle. He now knew how to love, and be loved by another.

Later in his life, Merton also came to terms with one of the challenges of a Type Four which is the ability to live in the moment. As his contemplative practice deepened, Merton discovered that if he could be open to the present moment that he could experience all aspects of life in that very moment. Suzanne Zuercher who wrote an Enneagram book about Merton writes:

> Another way of saying this is to acknowledge that Merton grew into a personal contemplative life, as distinct from merely being a member of a contemplative community. The journey by which he arrived at contemplation resulted in a

breakthrough from the surface elements of each moment to their deeper significance.[2]

At the end of his life, Merton made a trip to Asia where he was able to connect and meet with those who practiced Eastern religions. For some time, Merton had been exploring these ideas on his own, and in his writings, this could very well be his greatest contribution to contemporary spirituality. Personally, he noted the differences in Buddhism and Catholism, but with his Type Four view of the world, he was able to see and express that human experience is universal. Through his personal discovery, he could see the unity in the experiences of the Eastern and Western spiritual belief systems. In his own unique way, Merton created his own spiritual path encompassing these different beliefs. Tragically, he died a sudden death at only age 53 in Bangkok on his Asian trip. Luckily, his Asian journals were able to be printed so that everyone could share in the last few months of his life when he came to discover some of his most profound insights.

Through my first "Dark Night of the Soul", I discovered a new connection with spirituality. At age 34, I went through an early midlife crisis leaving behind a career which had left me feeling burned out on all levels – physically, emotionally, mentally and spiritually. Lucky for me, I found a medical doctor who also practiced some alternative methods. He suggested that I take up yoga since a lot of my physical issues appeared to be triggered by stress. He felt that the yoga would be a good exercise discipline as well as a stress reliever. My doctor never mentioned the spiritual benefits, but it was yoga that led me down a spiritual path. I had been raised as a Protestant, and had enjoyed going to church when I was younger, but I had given it up once I graduated from high school. The yoga opened my eyes to a new way of being religious by creating my own spiritual practice. I also began to delve into Eastern studies like Buddhism, and also more New Age practices like astrology and tarot. In my studies, I began to create my own spiritual path, and I began to slowly heal my physical body, my state of mind, and find an inner peace.

Now in my 40's, I have created my own spiritual path incorporating my beliefs in God, Goddess and Buddha. I read spiritual readings and meditate every day, and I incorporate many of the beliefs of those religions into my daily life. In my love of Mother Earth, I care for the earth in my own life by recycling, driving a hybrid, using solar power for electricity, supporting environmental causes and doing rituals to help heal the planet. I also do rituals around the phases of the Moon, and the seasons of the Earth. Through my study of Buddhism, I practice daily meditation, and include some of their beliefs in my daily life such as non-attachment, impermanence, and reincarnation. My belief in Christianity formed the foundation of my early life, and its roots are always with me even though my spiritual beliefs have evolved. For some people, one religious path works, and for others, we have to meld the paths together in our own creation.

It was my own personal journey as well as listening to other Romantics that revealed to me that feeding the soul is one of the keys to healing. In their own way, Romantics need to discover their reason for being, and their connection to the universe. Many Romantics do create their own spiritual paths. For them, it seems important to have their own unique connection with God, Goddess or Spirit. The spiritual connection seems to help them through some of the darkest days of life. Many people will set aside their meditation practices and spiritual communities when they get busy, but these spiritual tools can be as important as feeding our physical bodies, and breathing in clean air. Even if they don't believe in the God of organized religions, Romantics can take the time to go inward, and nurture their soul in the way that works best for them. A daily spiritual practice like walking in nature, journaling, meditating, praying, reading inspirational books and spending time in sacred places can be the first step in re-kindling that connection with Spirit.

Spiritual practices can be helpful for a Romantic on the healing path. In choosing a practice, it can be important to keep in mind the following suggestions: (1) Finding a practice that helps you to become more mindful and open to your life instead of actually supporting your illusions, (2) Selecting one that supports you in exploring some of the uncomfortable aspects and limitations of your personality, and (3) Choosing a method that encourages you to make up your own mind about your spiritual belief system.

Romantics need to find a spiritual belief system that meets their own unique set of needs. It is this system that can then become the foundation of their life. It can also help them to heal that original wound, to re-connect with their Self, and to find a deeper connection with their spirituality.

The connection can come from a solitary meditation practice included as part of their daily life. It could come from joining a spiritual community where the focus of life is on leading a spiritual life in all aspects of their life such as in their work, family, love relationships, etc. It can be joining a church or spiritual center which matches their spiritual beliefs allowing them to express their unique self while being part of a community.

In any case, the discovery of spirituality in their life appears to be an important healing component for a Romantic. For Jessamyn, it was a connection with Catholicism which led to a physical and spiritual healing. For Adia, it was her discovery of meditation, and her own connection with Spirit through the practice. For Cassie, it was discovering a spiritual community which was open to all spiritual beliefs, and combined Hinduism, Buddhism, Christianity, Judaism, Islam and nature-based religions in its weekly services. For Valerie, it was finding a spiritual center which included a large community of people with whom she could socialize and enjoy activities with outside of Sunday services. For Dee, it was going to spiritual services where they brought different practices together including meditation, chanting, prayers, music and group sharing.

The healing path itself can also be a spiritual path. In healing ourselves, we can help others heal around us. The magic and mystery of the healing process is different for each person as unique as their fingerprint. The wonder in the healing process is that our personal healing can have a ripple effect, and help others around us to heal. Through our own personal work, we can see how our family, friends, neighbors, co-workers and on and on are affected by our healing journey. That is the mystery of life – how we all seem to be connected on some level, and how we can affect one another with the changes that we make. We are not alone in our journey, but one of many who are here to learn lessons that help us grow and evolve as human and spiritual beings. We each have our own unique set of lessons, but as we work through the lessons we help others with their lessons. It is like we are all linked by a golden chain, and even when one of us stumbles and falls into that hole of despair, there is another person who can help us out, and guide us along on our path.

There are many healing tools to pick from on the healing path. They can be connected with the four elements of water, earth, fire and air. It is time to select which tools work best for you on the healing journey.

Chapter Nine: The Four Elements of Healing: Water, Earth, Fire and Air

The healing journey of the Romantic can be a winding path with a few steps forward, and then a backward turn, and then an appealing side path. It reminds me of the magical paths through the Hawaii Tropical Botanical Gardens north of Hilo on the Big Island of Hawaii. Through a splash of tropical color and green splendor, the paths wind their way through the gardens. Some paths lead to a bridge over a tropical stream to a mystical waterfall, and other paths lead down to the ocean with its black, lava rocks jutting into the sapphire blue waves. It reminds me of my healing journey. There were quiet times spent in deep contemplation on a bridge leading to the next path. There were also times I stood on a precipice of sharp rocks being tousled by the waves of life. I feel that the healing journey includes both inner times of quiet reflection, and also outward times in the fire burning with desire for a lover who helps us to transcend, or being led by a firewalker, a guide who has walked the path before us. The healing path is not a single path. For each person, it will involve different elements – some as splendid as a flower-filled meadow, and others as jarring as the rocky, lava roads of Hawaii. I don't believe that one path is better than the other, but I do believe that there are times when the rough terrain is the only way to go. It would be an ideal world if we could learn to embrace life in those sweet meadows, but we usually learn the hardest lessons in those lava fields of life.

My strongest suggestion is to find a guide to help you on your healing journey. The guide may be a professional therapist, a counselor, a healer, a coach or a body worker, but whoever they may be, find the guide that speaks to you.

Some "Guidelines" that I suggest: (1) Ask your friends for the names of guides that they may know, or have worked with. If you feel uncomfortable asking friends, then check with professional associations like the Marriage and Family Therapists, or Certified Massage Therapists. (2) Find a guide who shares enough similar beliefs as you, but is also different enough to challenge you and encourage you to push your edges. The closer you can come to an edge is where the learning will really begin. Your edge is a place outside your comfort zone where you feel stretched. It is in those edges where we can really grow and evolve on our life's path. It is human nature to want to stay with what is comfortable, but without those stretch marks, there is no real expansion of the Self. (3) Make a commitment to work with your guide for at least six months on a weekly basis. In committing to do the work, you are taking a stand to stay with the healing process even when it becomes challenging. It also means that you are giving you and your guide time to develop a sacred healing space. The longer you can commit to the work the better, but six months is a good starting point. (4) Practice self-care during this time period. Get enough sleep, eat nutritionally sound meals, exercise by doing something you enjoy, and make time for play each day even if it is just taking your dog for a walk – make it a playful time for you, too. (5) Peruse the four elements of healing tools in this chapter, and select at least one tool from each element to give yourself a sense of being balanced. For example, a Water tool could be working with Tarot cards to tap into your inner guidance; an Earth tool could be getting bodywork on a regular basis to help you be more in touch with your physical body; a Fire tool could be taking up belly dancing, and literally getting in touch with the fire in your belly; and an Air tool could be journaling about your healing process, your dreams or whatever comes up for you in doing this work.

There are no magic cures or healing potions on the path, but there are keys to unlock the secrets to your own personal healing. Others can tell you what you need to do to heal, but the deepest discoveries will come from within. It seems that it is a matter of timing when more than one key ingredient becomes available to you. For some of you, it began when you picked up this book, or took a class on the Enneagram Personality System, or joined a support group. Then, it's a matter of noticing the signs such as the letter in the mail about a class, or a friend mentioning a counselor, or a book being given to you by a friend. Look for the signs, and then follow them. There is usually more than one sign before we begin to wake up and pay attention to the message. Jung calls this synchronicity, a time when outer events resonate with an inner knowing. As you begin to notice the synchronicity in your everyday life, it will begin to happen more for you. There are no coincidences in life. Every event has a special meaning and purpose if we take the time to notice them. It is when our inner readiness for change meets the outer opportunity that we can then take that first step down the healing path. The following healing tools are meant to help you on that journey.

The Four Elements

The healing tools are represented by the four key elements of Water, Earth, Fire and Air. A balance of all four elements is essential for life, but most people are drawn to a couple of elements, and then may not feel connected to the other elements.

Water represents feelings, the deep well of emotions and moods, the mysteries of life, and the unconscious. The hidden parts of life are submerged in water from the womb where we are born to the healing power of the waters on this planet. Without water in our lives, we can be cut off from our feelings. We can be human "doings" instead of human "beings." The water can give us a deeper sense of our purpose in life. Without the water, we're not in touch with our intuition – that deep knowing that comes from within.

The earth is the ground, the soil, what we stand on, how we support ourselves in the world, and the way we manifest ideas into reality. We need Mother Earth to survive as a human race. We need to be in touch with the earth to remember where we came from – our ancestry, our roots, our very beginning, our birth are all part of the earth. The earth gives us inner strength and the security that comes from within. The earth is a reminder to be in the body, and to feel all the physical senses of living in a body. When we are connected with the earth, we are in tune with the Sun and the four seasons of winter, spring, summer and fall as well as the cycles of the Moon. The earth is how we ground ourselves in the world.

Fire symbolizes passion, drive, anger, creative energy – the spark of an idea is fire. It is the spark that inspires us to create and manifest an idea into reality. The spark is the beginning. It is the match that starts the fire, and inspires us to begin again in our lives. People that are drawn to fire can be outspoken, impulsive, expressive, passionate and exciting to be around. Romantics can express this fire in their passion for romance as well as in their desire to create art.

The air is our mental intellect, ideas, thoughts, and the way we can analyze and think through a problem. Air helps us to be objective, to make logical decisions, to share ideas with others and to come up with those brilliant ideas that lead to creation. Air is studying, reading, understanding – it inspires us with a thirst for knowledge. Air draws us to books, classes, discussions and other mental pursuits.

Hanalei Bay on Kauai, the Garden Island of Hawaii. Photograph by J. Alan Jackson.

Water Healing Tools

What element is a Romantic drawn to the most? The Romantic can probably get lost in the water element most often. They do have that longing, that attachment to intense feelings, and that natural intuition. They can become overly identified with their feelings where the feelings become who they are. The brooding poet, who writes melancholy sonnets is probably swimming in too much water. The love-struck woman who becomes addicted to the extraordinary highs of lovemaking, and avoids the more ordinary feelings is being swept away by water.

Romantics are very good at manipulating their feelings. They pick and choose which feelings they prefer while avoiding certain feelings. I can remember selecting some hauntingly, sad music when I was going through a heartbreak. I wanted to sink into my sadness. For a time, it is definitely okay to feel the loss, but to stay in it too long is to avoid the present moment. Romantics often

99

feel a sense of nostalgia about the past even the painful past. The Buddhists believe in allowing feelings to come up, feel them, and then let them go. They compare feelings to clouds that drift across the sky. The feeling comes over us, and then passes by without us getting attached to any one feeling. It can be a healthy exercise for a Romantic to notice when they get stuck in certain feelings, and then to practice releasing their hold on the feelings.

Water can also be a healing element for the Romantic. Literally immersing oneself in the water by taking baths, swimming in the ocean and rivers – the moving waters on this planet, and doing rituals with water can all be ways to use water to heal.

Since Romantics are naturally intuitive, there are ways to tap into that intuition to dip into it as if it is a pool of wisdom. One of the keys to healing is to tap into that inner guidance. The deep answers are within us. They are not found outside ourselves. Deep down, we know what we need to do, but our judgment can become clouded by the viewpoints of others. We have many voices in our heads – the voice of a parent, a teacher, a lover, a child and on and on. The voices can become so loud sometimes that we are unable to tune into our inner voice. This is when we need to make time to be alone, to be in solitude, and to retreat to a quiet place. It is in the solitude that we can find guidance and signs for the next step on our path. Personal retreats are excellent ways to tune into our own inner compass.

After I completed my counseling degree, I decided to go on a silent retreat at a Buddhist center high up in the Santa Cruz Mountains of California. I had just finished my final work for my master's degree, and I went there to celebrate my feeling of accomplishment. It really felt like a harvest time, and a peak experience in my life. At the center, I literally felt like I was on top of the world surrounded by the trees and this peaceful, contemplative world of the Buddhist monks. I felt like I had found my own personal nirvana on the planet. For three days, I decided to do my own version of a Native American vision quest. I was seeking guidance about my next step on my life's path. I spoke to no one, and had my meals delivered to my solitary cabin so I wasn't even surrounded by people at meal times. Each day, I took a symbolic hike where I would walk in silence, and notice the signs around me. I felt like I was the Greek Goddess, Artemis, the Goddess of the Hunt who loves nature and spends hours alone in the woods. I saw many animal signs – lizards, deer, hawks and other birds. But the only word that I saw on those walks was the single word "Keystone" on a rusty, crumpled beer can. At first, I walked right by it, and then I looked closer. After all, it was a sign even if it was on an empty beer can. I saw this sign long before I read the famous book, *The DaVinci Code* by Dan Brown. At first, I thought of Pennsylvania, the Keystone state, where I had lived for a few years in my 20's. Then I began to wonder about the word itself. Later, I told my husband about the sign, and he reminded me about the keystone being the center piece in a stone archway. Then, I looked up the word, *keystone* in my Webster's Dictionary, and the main definition was "the wedge-shaped piece at the crown of an arch that locks the other pieces in place."[1] Suddenly, this keystone seemed very important. It was holding the whole arch together. Without it, there wouldn't be an arch.

A whole year later, I read *The DaVinci Code* which was full of symbolism, but it was reading about the keystone that brought this sign back to my conscious mind. In the book, the leading character, Robert Langdon believes "The keystone is an encoded stone that lies beneath the sign of the Rose."[2] He also goes onto to describe it as an architectural term, "...Every stone archway requires a central, wedge-shaped stone at the top which locks the pieces together and carries all the weight. The stone is, in an architectural sense, the key to the vault."[3] And then lastly, "...the keystone is an encoded map...a map that reveals the hiding place of the Holy Grail."[4] It was the word map that caught my attention, and I began to wonder more about that sign that I had received on my solitary retreat. Was I being shown that there was a map that I could follow to find my next step?

Then almost a year later, I went on another personal retreat to a spiritual center in the East bay hills of the San Francisco Bay area of California. I had been to this center before, and had received many signs there. I decided to go on one of my symbolic walks through the woods. Again, I saw many beautiful, natural signs like deer, squirrels and birds. I even crossed a simple bridge made of utility poles stamped with the word, "High Voltage" which seemed to be a powerful message in itself. But it was the next sign that caught me by surprise. I was feeling completely open to the signs as I stepped into an open field with an expansive view. The view was grand taking in Mount Diablo, and stretching all the way from Vallejo and back down Freeway 680 which was way off in the distance.

Admiring this view and thinking of the lucky landowner who owned this piece of prime real estate, I neglected to look down until I turned back to walk down the same path. Then I noticed the sign – a single beer can with the words "Keystone Light" shining in the sun. But then I looked around the whole field, and there was a whole case of "Keystone Light" beer cans spread all over the grass from some late-night party. I began to smile and laugh out loud. It was like the universe didn't want me to miss the sign of a single can so they left me a field full of signs, and even the empty cardboard box. This time the message was clear. The keystone had become a light, a beacon for me shining on my next step. For the rest of my time there, I received other signs, and they all seemed to be pointing me in the direction of writing this book on the Romantic. The "Keystone Light" guided me to the book, and the book became like a keystone – a map of healing for Romantics.

I began to wonder. Could there be a map that a Romantic could follow? With clues leading them to their healing path? Could one of the clues be turning inward? Asking yourself the question, "What is my inner guidance telling me?" It requires patience, and the ability to stay in the place of not knowing until the answers come. In our world of quick fixes and easy solutions, it can be challenging to stay in this place of murky waters. But a temporary fix would be like putting a band-aid over a deeper wound. It might help for a short while, but in the long run, the bleeding would begin again.

At this stage, divination tools can be helpful. The symbolic nature of Tarot cards, I Ching coins, and Runes can shed light on the messages of our unconscious. The unconscious speaks to us in symbols, images and colors like in our nighttime dreams. The messages are often not direct, but indirect, and they are not logical, but intuitive. Intuition is yin energy – receptive, watery, and still. The messages can rise to the surface like a lotus breaking through the water with its silky, wet blossom. The lotus flower comes from a muddy birth, and lies hidden beneath the murky waters, and is only seen when it surfaces to reveal its white, pristine beauty. Like the lotus, the messages can lie hidden, and unexpectedly surface when we are ready to hear them.

Any tools that work with symbols can be key at this point such as dream work, and astrology. You may also be drawn to seeking out a psychic or a medium, and they may give you guidance on your journey. The higher use of this information is to realize that the choice and life direction that you take are still up to you. The psychics and mediums cannot tell you what to do, and if they do try to direct you in your life, I would suggest being very discerning and selective about what you do with their information. You still hold the key to your own healing. Listen to your own heart, and what feels right for you. No one else knows better than you what is right for you at any given moment in time. Guidance can be helpful, but we often get clouded by others' expectations and direction for us. It is always wise to step back, and go within to find the deeper truth. We are often surprised to learn that we were always holding the key to the challenge we have been facing. Romantics can discover that they are like a Zen koan knowing the answer to their own personal riddle.

Donna M. Fisher-Jackson, M.A.

Half Dome in Yosemite National Park in California. Photograph
by J. Alan Jackson.

Earth Healing Tools

The healing knowledge of the Earth can also be a healing
element for the Romantic. Getting grounded in their bodies can

be a serious challenge for them. More likely to be up in the clouds or lost in their feelings, they are often out of touch with their physical body and its' needs. Basic grounding techniques can be key for a Romantic. Through guided meditations and visualizations, they can learn how to ground the energy through their feet into the Earth. Other simple grounding techniques include eating grounding foods like cereal, oatmeal, breads, and meat. When you feel light-headed, choosing a grounding food instead of coffee or sweets can be helpful. Bodywork such as massage, energetic healing and body-oriented psychotherapies can be very healing for a Romantic, and help them to re-connect with their physical body. They do need guidance to spend more time in their bodies rather than in their imagination dreaming of a life they would like to lead in the far-off future.

Being fully present is another key piece in the healing for the Romantic. The longing to be somewhere else takes them out of present time, and also uses up a lot of energy. Think of your energy as a full tank of gas. If you spend half that tank on longing to be somewhere else, then you are left only with half a tank of gas for your current life. The loss of energy can hinder you from living fully. You may not have the energy to exercise, take classes, attend social events or even to just do the daily tasks of life. This is when you need to take a serious look at your life, and how you are spending your energy. It's also a time to look and see where you can make changes, and accept what you are unable to change. As human beings, we can spend a great deal of energy worrying about things like the weather, the traffic, politics – knowing that in the moment, there is nothing that we can really change at this time, and how much easier on ourselves it would be to accept and surrender to the moment. Make the changes we can about our corner of the world– take an umbrella on a rainy day, drive during off-peak hours when we can, and support the politicians that we do believe in.

The time spent in longing and daydreaming can seriously keep a Romantic from moving forward in their lives. A certain amount of daydreaming is natural, and helpful to tap into our right brain and our creative juices, but if we spend too much time there, then we are really missing the experience of living on this planet, and being fully alive in our physical bodies.

For Jessamyn, daydreaming was a full-time occupation for a certain time in her life. She could spend hours in her own world-reading spiritual books, communicating with friends via e-mail, and talking on the phone to her long-distance lover. During that time of her life, she had little connection with the "real" world, and only left her mountain-top home to do her volunteer work, run some errands, and to visit friends. It was almost a hard adjustment for her to be in the "real" world with the traffic, loud people, un-comfortable restaurants and the mundane world. She had literally risen above the world living in her home in the hills, and had little desire to be immersed in the world below. It was only when she left her husband, and her mountain-top home that she was thrust into the "real" world. Even after a few years of separation from her husband, she is still struggling to live alone, and make her way in the world. Now, she has to pay attention to what she spends her money on. Now, she realizes the challenges of being grounded and finding time for her creative pursuits. She is fortunate to have a creative profession which allows her a flexible schedule, but the reality is that her income only affords her a simple lifestyle. She misses her more lavish lifestyle, and spends time longing for her old life and wishing that she was living somewhere else. The longing keeps her from being present in her new life, and from moving forward. It saps her energy, and she complains of feeling listless and tired a lot of the time. A subtle shift in her attention from the longing to being here now could make a big difference.

We can find ourselves having a lot more energy for our present life if we can make that shift to now. It is easier to be in the moment when we like the moment like on a balmy day on a tropical island. But try this mental exercise on a cloudy, rainy day at home. Sink into the experience, feel the rain, really observe the rain as it falls landing on the ground creating puddles. Watch it as it bounces off the pavement. Accept the rain. Be present with the rain. No other moment exists, but the rain coming down. This exercise even for 15 minutes can free you up from so much. You don't have to worry about what's coming up next, or what you have to do next on your "To Do" List. Write it down on your "To Do" List, then let it go until you need to do it, and then give it your full attention when it's time. Being fully present is another key ingredient for healing for the Romantic.

Eating a healthy diet can also be crucial for a Romantic. Drawn to the intensity of emotions, Romantics can be prone to mood swings. Some of these mood swings can be triggered by diet. They can be drawn to rich foods and sweets to comfort themselves. They can also abuse alcohol and drugs to alter their moods. Professional counseling is very important when there is any kind of alcohol and drug abuse. There are also support groups for overeating, alcohol and drug addiction. A professional nutritionist can also be a good guide on healthier diet choices. A healthy self-discipline can be key for a Romantic from getting sufficient sleep, getting regular exercise and working regular hours. It can be easy for them to get off track when they are not getting enough sleep or eating right.

Connecting to the earth in simple ways such as gardening, hiking, and following the seasons can help a Romantic to have a more wholesome discipline. The physical body has a way of getting our attention when we are out of balance. We usually get a message that we are out of balance first mentally, then emotionally, and lastly in the physical body. If we are not paying attention to the earlier messages, then it can result in a physical illness. Many well-known healing professionals such as Louise Hay and Dr. Christiane Northrup have written books about the power of the mind-body connection, and how "dis-ease" comes from a breakdown in this connection. For example, I have often been challenged with being flexible. It can be easy for me to get stuck in a place of structure and rigidity. I like my daily routines, and do change them at times, but I have noticed that when I have had to make changes last minute in my daily schedule that I can become resistant and upset. My flexibility was tested, and I noticed that I could become very rigid. In my physical body, the rigidity has shown up as stiffness in my joints, tightness in my jaw, and a stiff neck. It was as if my own rigid thinking had caused the rigidity in my physical body. Since noticing these signs in my body, I have begun to do yoga more often to be more flexible in my body, and I have also noticed that it has created more flexible thinking as well. The physical changes in our bodies are another key way that we can receive messages.

The healing balm of nature is one of the key healing tools of the earth. If they can tap into the goddess energy of Artemis, the Goddess of the Hunt, they can experience the healing touch of nature by walking on a beach, hiking a mountain trail, or spending time in a park. Being outdoors can give a Romantic a sense of the bigger picture of life. It can help them to be less self-absorbed, and connect with a larger sense of the universe. Being in nature can also help them to get in touch with the seasons, and begin to work with them in their own life.

Through following the seasons of the Earth, and the cycles of the Moon, they can begin to see that there is a season and a cycle at work in their own lives. Beginning anew in the springtime is a lot easier with the support of the universe. Begin any new project like your healing journey in the spring time, and you can just feel the earth welling up with its greenness to help you heal. Then in the summer, you can begin to bloom with your new awareness. Each new insight will feel like a new blossom that you can add to your bouquet of knowledge. The summer is a time to get in touch with your inner child once again. It is the time to play and celebrate life. As you approach the fall, you can feel the abundance- the fruits of your labors. You are ready to reap the rewards, and harvest all the wisdom that you have gathered on your journey. The summer and fall are more extraverted times where you can be outdoors more often, and involved in more active pursuits of healing like hiking, swimming and being out in nature. With the approaching winter, you can prepare for your inward healing time. You can immerse yourself in your journals, your healing books, and other healing tools like bodywork. You can warm yourself in front of the fire, and contemplate all the knowledge and experiences that you have gathered over the year. After the holidays, it can be a time to do a silent retreat, and to prepare your plans for the coming New Year. Though, the winter is a dormant time – not for planting seeds, but for gathering the seeds of new projects that you can release into the rich, black soil of spring.

The Moon cycles can also be utilized every month for a shorter cycle of 28 days where we can begin new projects, and see them to fruition. The New Moon, being like spring, is the time to release our intentions and plans for the coming month. The First Quarter Moon to the Full Moon is like summer where you can work on those intentions and begin to develop them further. The Full Moon to the Last Quarter Moon is like the harvest of fall. The light of the Moon now reveals what you have achieved and gathered during this cycle. You can then decide whether or not it is time to let go of a certain project, or to set it aside for the next Moon cycle. During the Last Quarter of the Moon, the final phase of the cycle, it is like winter time. It is a time of reflection, of endings, of finishing up the project, or at least completing the first stage, and preparing for the next step. Then, when the New Moon arrives, you can begin once again with your intentions and plans for the next Moon cycle.

The power of the Moon cycles has helped me with many projects including writing this book, and has also given me insight when it is time to let go, and wait for the next project to reveal itself. It is a very feminine/yin process of being and contemplating which can feel very different from the masculine/yang energy of doing and achieving. Working with the Moon cycles is more of a waiting and going within to follow your own inner guidance on the right, next step. But it also involves, showing up to do the work, and trusting that you are being guided in the process. It can also lead to a deeper awareness then if you rushed headlong into the active doing.

Donna M. Fisher-Jackson, M.A.

Summer Fireworks. Photograph by J. Alan Jackson.

Fire Healing Tools

The healing tools of fire all come from the sacred center of passion and creativity. Romantics are naturally passionate and intense in their romantic affairs. For them, they probably need to learn to channel this flame of desire into creative projects as well. Naturally creative, Romantics need an outlet for their creativity such as painting, writing, music, dancing, and any activity that allows them to tap into their creative well. For Romantics who are out of touch with their creativity, there are good resource books such as *The Artist's Way, The Vein of Gold, Walking in this World,* and most recently, *Finding Water,* all by Julia Cameron. These books are a personal journey of creative exploration presented in a 12-week format where there is reading, special tasks, and journaling for each week. In the process of tapping into their personal creativity, a Romantic could uncover their deeper issues that are keeping them from expressing their true Self. The benefits of working with the books in a group is the sharing of personal experiences with oth-

110

ers, and the revealing of deep feelings, which can be very healing for a Romantic who tends to be too self-absorbed and withdrawn from others. I have personally been through the books more than once with a group, and I highly recommend them. Cameron's writing is exquisite, and most Romantics would enjoy the deep, unconscious exploration that she encourages in her exercises.

Art therapy, another avenue for creativity, could be very healing for a Romantic. Naturally drawn to the creative arts, they could enjoy drawing mandalas, painting, clay sculpting, collage-making and any other tools of art therapy. It can be an excellent way for them to get out of their head, and spend some time with a tactile tool like art work. It can also help them to tap into deeper places in their psyche that they might find hard to express in words, but could express symbolically in their art.

Chakra work may also be a way to tap into one's creativity. The chakras are our energy centers that connect us with different qualities of our Being. Most Romantics need some healing in the area of the second chakra. The second chakra is our source of creativity and sexuality. It is why we feel a desire to create through our sexuality by giving birth to a child, but we can also give birth to other creative projects. The second chakra is where we hold our creative power. Through energy work or personal healing work, we can learn to get in touch with this power. The second chakra is located near our naval, but it is not something that we can visually see with our eyes, but we can sense it within our bodies. It is also the area where we store our emotions, and the home of our inner child. Many people need to do work in this area of their body because of the inner child. If we had a perfect childhood, there would be no wounded parts to look at, but most Romantics have gone through some suffering in their childhood that they need to address. In getting in touch with this inner child, we can also release our innate creativity. Connect with your inner child in playful ways like with finger-painting, freestyle dancing, jumping rope, playing with jacks, or any other games that remind you of your childhood. Of course, for a more serious wounding like child abuse, I strongly suggest working with a counselor trained in working with abuse issues who can guide you through your healing process. Chakra work with an energy healer, can help you to get in touch with your energetic bodies that also affect your well-being in your physical body.

Movement practices such as dancing, kundalini yoga, and aerobics can be a good way for Romantics to feel the fire in their belly. The movement helps them to get out of their heads, and to tap into their fire. The compact music disc, *Initiation*, by Gabrielle Roth and the Mirrors is an excellent way to get moving, and to process deep feelings without having to always talk about them. Roth's Five Rhythms movement exercises are offered on compact discs, and there are parts of the country where people have movement dances where they incorporate her work. It can be very freeing and stimulating for a Romantic to share the experience with a group.

Sound healing can also be another avenue to help you bring up your fire, and connect you with your self-expression. There are many sound healing tools including crystal bowls, Tibetan singing bowls, chanting, and singing. Experiencing healing sounds, or using your own voice to make healing sounds can help you to connect with a deeper level of your Self. Some people are more in tune with sound, and often recall memories through music and even dream night-time dreams that contain music. For them, sound healing could be an ideal healing tool.

Romantics also need to use their inner fire to initiate more in their lives. They can tend to spend time in self-absorbed activities, and dream of the life they would like to lead. Taking that first step to creating that life can make it more real. The taking action can also build self-confidence. Romantics can often feel like they are not quite ready to take on a new challenge or activity, but sometimes, they just need to take that first step. Once, they start to have positive experiences with that practice, then they begin to feel like they can initiate more in their lives. Taking risks is cultivating the fire within. The more healthier risks they take, then they can learn to feel better about themselves. It is a positive self-fulfilling prophecy.

Meaningful work seems to be another key for a Romantic. If they are able to do work that they enjoy, and that helps others in some way, then their life can be greatly enhanced. Helping others helps Romantics to be less self-absorbed. Through their work, they can discover their Self along with using their unique gifts to help others. Many people call this right livelihood where our gifts and talents are able to be expressed through our work in the world.

For a Romantic, finding that career path that utilizes their unique gifts and helps others in the process can make a huge difference in how they view life. Being connected to the real world through their work while using their innate talents can help a Romantic to discover the inner happiness that they have been seeking through other means. Romantics are often found working in creative and innovative careers. If they are doing a more practical job, it is often seen as a necessity to supporting their real work such as an artist working as a waitress at night to pay the bills. Some career paths that are attractive to Romantics include all artistic endeavors such as writers, artists, musicians, dancers, interior decorators, etc., They may also pursue healing careers such as body workers, counselors, intuitives, and mediums where they are the deep sea divers of the unconscious. They can also be gifted wounded healers. If they can heal from their own pain, then they can in turn help others face their pain. They also make excellent hospice volunteers because they are not afraid to talk about death. They can also help others with addictions having faced their own inner demons. They enjoy working for causes that they believe in like the environment, feminism, animal rights, etc. They often lead unconventional lifestyles, and follow non-conformist paths in their work.

It is challenging for a Romantic to fit into a traditional box with the corporate job, the traditional partner with the suburban home and the 2.5 children. They may try to play that role for a while, but it usually doesn't fit too well. Like the feel of wearing clothes that are too tight, they will break through the seams, stretch the fabric of their lives and create a whole new design that uniquely fits them. Others may find them too avante garde, or too experimental, or a little crazy, but they definitely have to follow an inner calling all their own. If they have a strong sense of Self, they will often follow their own creative path from an early age, but if they have low self-esteem as a child, then they may follow what others want from them until they wake up one day like from a bad dream, and realize they have been living someone else's life, then they will break through the illusion, take that leap of faith, and venture into the unknown to create a life that speaks to their soul.

Each personal life story in this book reveals that uniqueness and that strong individuality which are truly the gifts of the Romantic. They are here to share their gifts with others, but they often get lost in their deep soul searching where they lose track of the higher purpose of their life. It is helpful for them to get in touch with that life purpose, but it is also important for them to take it one step further, and share this gift with the world.

Discovering those unique gifts that they have, and then using them in their work can be one of the most important keys to the healing path of a Romantic.

Bristlecone Pines in the White Mountains of the Inyo National
Forest in Bishop, CA.
Photograph by J. Alan Jackson.

Air Healing Tools

Seeking higher knowledge is an air tool that can help us discover the big picture of life. There are times in our healing process when we can use our minds to gather information, to be more present, and to be more balanced.

Everyone has different ways of gathering knowledge whether it is taking classes, reading books, listening to tapes, watching videos or joining support groups. It is good if you find the avenue that works best for you. The key is to discover the right tool for you, and then to head down that path. There will be some fear and resistance as you stretch into new territory, but know that you are not alone in these feelings. All of us will find at times excuses and reasons to not take that class, read that book, or join that group, but in the end, we are only holding ourselves back from our own personal growth. Believe me, as you stretch yourself, it does get

115

easier at times. It is like exercising a muscle. Once, you begin to use the muscle, then it is not so painful each time. And eventually, it becomes easier until you are ready to reach further again. If you can stretch yourself, and get past that uncomfortable feeling, you can find a wealth of knowledge that can help you on your healing path.

Choosing an air healing tool is not meant to distract you from your thoughts, but to put you smack in the middle of your experience right now. Being fully present is one of the daily challenges of a Romantic. With a tendency to long for the past and dream about the future, they can have trouble being with what is going on in the moment right now. It is also tied to their avoidance of the ordinary. If the moment is an ordinary one like doing laundry or cleaning the house, they can avoid the task altogether, or dream their way through it. The Romantic tends to feel fully alive when they are experiencing a heightened experience like sharing an intense conversation with a friend, or a passionate encounter with a lover. Those moments are more extraordinary than ordinary, and they would rather spend time creating those moments than dealing with the tasks of everyday life.

There are some practices that a Romantic could utilize to live more in the present, and be more accepting of the ordinary. They could study meditation where they can learn to ground, center and focus their attention in the moment. Grounding is to become fully present in your body as was discussed under the earth healing tools.

Centering is to find your personal center. Some people suggest placing your finger near your navel, and focusing on that point in your body to find your personal center. When you are centered, others can not pull you off center. Being centered is like having the rudder of your sailboat in the water. Without a rudder, a sailboat sails aimlessly without any direction, and can be easily blown off course by a passing wind. When we are centered, then we have a clear sense of direction, but also are flexible enough to receive new information as it comes in and make adjustments to our course. We can then choose consciously which wind to follow instead of going around in circles. Having a strong center affects us on all levels – mentally with clear, conscious thinking; emotionally – feeling the emotions, but not being swept away by them; physically – having a sense of our physical body, and being able to nurture ourselves; and spiritually – having a sense of purpose in our lives and a deeper connection with the divine whatever that means for us.

Focusing your attention in the moment is to be present with all of your senses allowing the thoughts and feelings to come and go. Be observing, and also receptive. In that deep place of being present, we can often receive insights and messages. It is also the place to release intentions, or to pray.

There are many kinds of meditation connected with different spiritual paths. Many of the Eastern religions include meditation as part of their spiritual practice. There are also ways to use journaling and art as a meditative practice. The idea is to write or paint being in the moment with whatever thoughts and feelings are arising. There is also walking meditation where we walk in silence being open to our experience in each purposeful step.

Journaling is also one of the key air healing tools. Keeping a diary or journal can help us to express what may be hard to speak openly to a friend or a guide. In our writing, we can give ourselves permission to fully express our deepest desires, wishes, pain, challenges and experiences. If you can keep your writing private by keeping it in a safe place, you will then feel freer to express all parts of your Self. Julia Cameron of *The Artist's Way* suggests journaling everyday which she calls morning pages. During the 12 week healing program in her books, she suggests doing morning pages every day. The morning pages include three pages daily of longhand writing in the morning. The writing is longhand because it helps you to tap into the right side of your brain as well as the left side. It is also to be done in the morning when your mind is fresh, and hopefully not cluttered with the previous day's events. In the morning pages, you can write about whatever your heart desires. You can write the same phrase over and over until you open up into something new. Most people do find resistance in the beginning to the idea of having to write every morning, but then as time goes by, they usually find the words flowing more, and they feel more ready to write when they sit down with their pen and paper. The writing helps you to connect with your inner guidance, and to uncover what is really going on beneath your everyday life.

Natalie Goldberg of *Writing down the Bones* and other writing books is a big advocate of writing practice. In her writing practice, you can pick a topic, or begin with a phrase like "I remember..", and then the idea is to just write for ten minutes straight. You can go longer, but 10 minutes is a good starting point. The idea is to literally practice at writing, but I have also found that it is a great technique to get to the bottom of what is going on for you at any given moment. You may start out writing about ice cream, but then somehow, you find yourself in the middle of that argument you had with your boss, and then you go deeper into what is really bothering you. It is a great uncovering technique to get in touch with your thoughts and feelings below the conscious mind. For anyone who struggles with journaling, this can be an excellent way to get jumpstarted. Goldberg's books have all kinds of suggestions such as what to write about as well as how to demystify the creative process.

Carl Jung's approach to psychology, and many of his tools such as working with the archetypal energies may appeal to a Romantic. Their natural gifts of intuition and imagination can be very helpful in this kind of work. They would enjoy exploring the archetypes that they identify with most especially the goddess archetypes like Aphrodite, Artemis, Athena, Demeter, Hera, Hestia and Persephone. The Romantic may identify most with Aphrodite, the Goddess of Love. When Aphrodite is present as the main archetype in a woman's personality, she may fall in love often and easily—a common theme for a Romantic. Jungian analyst, Jean Shinoda Bolen describes the experience of an Aphrodite woman eloquently in her passage on falling in love:

> When two people fall in love, each sees the other in a special, enhancing (Aphrodite-golden) light and is drawn toward the other's beauty. There is magic in the air; a state of enchant-

ment or infatuation is evoked. Each feels beautiful, special, more godlike or goddess like than their ordinary selves...An Aphrodite woman may go through a series of intense love affairs, swept up each time by the magic (or archetypal) experience of being in love. To end this pattern, she must learn to love someone "someone warts and all" someone who is an imperfect human rather than a God.[5]

There are a handful of books on the gods and goddesses that I would recommend. Bolen has written two amazing books, *Goddesses in Every Woman* and *Gods in Every Man,* which help you explore how these archetypes are alive in your own life, and in your romantic partners. Another insightful book on the goddesses is *The Goddess Within* by Jennifer Barker Woolger and Roger J. Woolger which even includes a questionnaire to discover which goddesses that you most relate to, and how to integrate more of the missing goddesses into your life. (Refer to Appendix D for more in-depth descriptions of the seven Greek goddess archetypes.)

The idea behind exploring these goddess and god archetypes is to become conscious of how they are influencing us in our lives. If we are unaware of them, they can then steer us down life paths with little or no awareness that we are being led astray. For example, a woman who is out of touch with her Demeter, the Mother Goddess, archetype could find herself forgetting to use her birth control in a casual relationship. Her unconscious desire to have a baby could be so strong, but she may be out of touch with that part of herself until she finds herself pregnant by accident. If she could allow herself to feel the ticking of her biological clock, then she could make a conscious decision to have a child with a more suitable partner. Becoming aware of Demeter in herself can bring awareness and healing around the issue of becoming a Mother.

As Adia followed her heart, she became caught up in the desires of the goddess, Aphrodite. Adia loved her new creative work place, and her new sexy clothing, but unconsciously she wanted more. She wanted to be in love, and feel those heights of passion once again. It was this calling from the goddess that led Adia down the path of love's illusion. It didn't take long for Adia to attract a lover, who saw that starry-eyed look in her eyes. Adia could blame the goddess of love for leading her astray, but really she only had herself to blame. If she had been able to face what was missing in her marriage and in her life, and share her feelings with her husband, then she could have made a more conscious choice in relationship. Because she was not aware of her deep desires and afraid to rock the boat in her marriage, she ended up looking outside her relationship to satisfy her longing. Of course, the romance and passion of an affair can be intoxicating, but then, she eventually had to deal with the painful consequences of her actions. If she had been aware of how to work with the goddess energy, she could have brought that energy into her own marriage, and into creative outlets. Adia may also have benefited from working with some of the other goddesses like Hera, the goddess of marriage, and Athena, the warrior goddess to help develop other sides of herself for balance rather than focusing so much energy on the desires of the Goddess of Love.

As Zweig and Wolf write in *Romancing the Shadow*, "Affairs reflect an imbalance in the primary relationship and can be used to compensate for a missing element: freedom, passion, spirituality, creative inspiration, masculine or feminine energies. Thus a god – Eros, Aphrodite, Dionysus, Artemis – who has been sacrificed in the marriage reappears in the affair, bringing feelings of expansion and delight."[6]

Adia didn't feel like she could express her sensual, romantic side in the marriage. She had a split image of being a wife. There was the "good wife" who wouldn't be overly sexual, but more subdued and always pleasing others, and then the "bad wife" who would seek out a secret affair to satisfy her romantic longings. Since she didn't feel like she could talk to her husband about these sexual desires, she looked outside her marriage for the solution. Zweig and Wolf write, "An affair in general, and sex in particular, can obscure the primary relationship's deeper problems, acting as camouflage by becoming the apparent problem so that the underlying root issues go unnoticed. Like an addiction that appears to be the problem while camouflaging the shadow's deeper needs, an

120

affair may divert the attention from the less-visible developmental crisis in the relationship."[7]

In retrospect if Adia had been conscious of the influence of Aphrodite, she could have chosen not to act out the affair, but instead to see her sexual desires for another man as a wake-up call in her own marriage. She needed to take a chance at expressing her real needs in the relationship in order to move to a new level of relationship with her husband. She needed to heal this split in herself between the "good wife" and the "bad wife", and feel like she could express her whole Self in the marriage. As Zweig and Wolf write, "By uncovering who is motivating an affair (which god or goddess) and what this character is telling us, we may learn to meet its deeper needs, preferably without unconsciously destroying an ongoing relationship. Or we can choose more consciously to end a relationship without the pain of betrayal."[8]

Of course, this is challenging work to do alone, and a guide like a therapist or counselor could really be important in the healing process. Adia did eventually find herself a counselor, and began the healing journey first alone, and then with her husband.

Another Jungian tool is working with our dreams which could also be considered a water tool since we are retrieving messages from the deep sea of the unconscious. Dreamwork can be appealing to a Romantic because they are often very in tune with their nighttime dreams, and can enjoy keeping a dream diary, and exploring the symbols of the dreams. Dreams are messages from our unconscious. They can be dreams about our daily events, and how we are trying to work through some issues. They can also be dreams of our future plans. They can involve relationships, and in other cases, we can encounter shadow sides of ourselves that we are not yet conscious of in our everyday life. In our nighttime dreams, Jung also believed that we could tap into the collective unconscious, which is made up of all the symbols and experiences that we share as a human race. Some of these dreams could include ancient symbols like the cross, the five-pointed star, or religious deities that have meaning for us.

Donna M. Fisher-Jackson, M.A.

There are many methods at remembering dreams. Before, you go to sleep you can focus on your intention to remember your dreams. Then when you awake in the night, you can have a note-pad and pen next to your bed where you can jot down those first impressions. Some people find that this wakes them up too much from the dream so you could just try writing important fragments of the dream, and hope that you can put the pieces together in the morning.

Then through journaling, you can write out the dream as much as you can remember with as much detail as possible. At this point, the Jungian approach is to ask yourself questions about the dream such as: What are you doing in the dream?; How does it feel in the dream?; What issues and situations are unresolved in the dream?; What symbols in the dream are important to you?; What relation does this dream have to your everyday life at this time?; What is the healing force in this dream?. The Jungian approach also includes exploring the dream without looking up the symbols in dream dictionaries. The belief is that the symbol has a personal meaning, and a universal meaning. For example, some people may see a black cat in their dream as a positive sign because they have a black cat as a pet, and others may see it as a symbol of bad luck. It is probably wise to first figure out the symbols for yourself, and then you can always look at a dream dictionary if you feel inspired to know more.

Romantics also may enjoy working with dreams with a group. You could create your own dream circle with friends, or find a dream group in your area. If you do decide to create a dream cir-cle, honor the sacredness of what you are doing. Create a safe, sacred space where what is spoken in the circle remains in the circle. You could use rituals such as lighting candles or incense to tap more into the altered state of the dream time. Some guidelines that you could follow are (1) The dreamer tells their dream with no interruptions. (2) The members of the group then ask questions to get more insight into the dream, but they refrain from interpret-ing the dream. The questions help the dreamer to explore their dream further for themselves. (3) The dreamer then re-reads their dream. (4) Each member now responds as if the dream was their own. For example, "If it were my dream..." (5) Then the dreamer expresses what they feel the dream means to them. The dream circle allows the dreamer to come to their own interpretation of the dream, but the input from the other members can often trigger a memory or deeper insight into the dream.[9] You could coordinate your dream circle with the cycles of the Moon. Try holding your circle on the New Moon or the Full Moon to get a sense of what day works best for your group as a whole. Once, you begin to work with dreams, then it can become a valuable tool for connecting with your unconscious, and the larger picture of your life. Guidance and insight can come from your dreams that can help you on your healing path.

Hypnotherapy is also another amazing tool that works with the sub-conscious. In this hypnotic state, we are able to make changes at a deep, sub-conscious level. We all take in core beliefs as young children when we are not able to filter them out. These beliefs become deeply embedded in our sub-conscious mind, and can direct us in our lives without our conscious awareness. With the help of a certified hypnotherapist, we can begin to uncover these core beliefs, and change them, and begin to make positive changes in our lives. For example, some young children heard statements which they internalized as "not being worthy of love," or "not being good enough." As they grow up, they carry these unconscious beliefs into their adult relationships by attracting partners who mirror the belief of "not being worthy of love" back to them, or they create circumstances like not finishing college that show them that they are "not good enough." Under hypnosis, these core beliefs can literally be re-written with amazing results in their everyday lives. Sometimes, we really do want to change, but there can be unconscious beliefs that keep us from changing. Hypnotherapy is one tool that can help us change at this deep level.

All these different healing tools can help us at different times on our life paths. If you pick and choose them from the different elements, you can bring more balance and awareness to your life. And so the healing journey continues.

☙❧

Chapter Ten: The Conscious Evolution of the Four

At some point in my own healing journey, I realized that there is no end destination, or a moment when I will be "all done," and be completely healed. Like most journeys in life, the real learning comes from the journey rather than the final destination. There will be times in life when you take a break from the intensive healing work, and get off the train, and enjoy the scenery. But once, you are committed to growing and evolving in this life, then you will find yourself feeling ready to get back on the train, and continue the journey of learning.

For me, I find a sense of peace in knowing that I am on my path, and I am making changes to heal myself. I also realize that I am whole and complete right at this moment in time. We, Romantics, are known for focusing on what is missing in our Selves, and in our lives, but when we can stop and take a look, and see all the positive qualities and experiences that we have in our lives, then we can deepen our awareness.

I also came to the realization that I have all the time in the world to do this soul work. If you believe in more than one lifetime, there is a freedom in knowing that you don't have "to do it all" this lifetime. Every lesson that you learn, and every new awareness that you receive takes you one step closer to living your life from the center of your whole Self. It's when we stop growing, and refuse to change our familiar ways that we begin to age. Growing and continually stretching ourselves can literally keep us feeling younger on many levels. It could very well be the elixir of the fountain of youth. I have met women who are well past 60 in their physical age, but who radiate an inner beauty and youthfulness that makes them seem so much younger. They are women who are committed to a path of evolution, and through their own inner and outer work, they continue to grow on so many levels. Without face lifts and expensive plastic surgery, they maintain a feeling of youth from their own inner work. That could be an important lesson for a Romantic who may be looking outside themselves for the key to looking younger when it already is in their possession within their Self.

If there is one prescription that I could make to stay young is to keep on learning and growing in some aspect of your life. Take up a new hobby. Sign up for that dance class. Try eating new foods. Travel to a new place. It seems that the stretching of our souls can keep us flexible in mind, body and spirit.

For me, the healing journey continues. With more awareness, I don't fall into my old habits as easily, and when I do, I am able to make a different choice. I don't have to go down that path with the potholes anymore. I am able to go down a new path which has its own new set of challenges, but now, I expect to find those challenges. I don't expect to ever be "all done" with my learning, or my healing work. There are times when I am leading a quieter and more inward life, and then there are times when I am more outer-directed and busy with my external life. Now, I am more accepting of these different cycles of life as I get glimpses of the big picture of life. In a more inward phase, I am writing this book, and then when it is published, I will move into a more outer phase of promoting the book. They are both part of my life, and a natural progression of the cycles of life. Now, I am making more conscious choices in my life.

In the Enneagram system, living more consciously is following your Direction of Integration. Instead of reacting unconsciously and living through their personality, a person makes a conscious choice to live life more fully, to let go of old habits, and to live more with the truth of their whole Self. The Enneagram system shows it as a natural process of unfolding as a person lets go of defenses, attitudes and fears. As Riso and Hudson write, "A tree does not have to do anything to go from a bud to a flower to a fruit: it is an organic, natural process, and the soul wants to unfold in the same way. The Enneagram describes this organic process in each type."[1]

Healthy Fours move on their path of integration by incorporating the healthy aspects of a Type One, The Perfectionist/The Reformer. These Fours engage with reality through meaningful action. By committing themselves to principles and activities beyond their subjective world, Fours discover who they are, and become more accepting of their flaws. They realize that self-expression does not mean indulging in moods, but become more self-disciplined by working consistently to contribute something worthwhile to their world. No longer aloof bystanders, they participate more fully in their lives, and develop a stronger sense of themselves through work and their connections with others.[2] Like Jessamyn who is now more on that path of integration by practicing her music on a regular basis, and by sharing her music with others through performances, recordings and teaching.

Not needing to identity with the critical side of an average Type One, a Four's higher expression of a One is to practice discernment in where they decide to focus their attention. It is also working with acceptance at all levels. It means self-acceptance, acceptance of others, and acceptance of the reality of a situation, which leads to more mutually satisfying relationships with others. On this path, Fours learn to build a more lasting sense of identity and self-esteem because it is based more in reality rather than on their imagination or transient emotional states. As they discover qualities in themselves that were once invisible, Fours connect in a deep way with their true identity. They are able to let go of a self image where they believe they are more flawed than others, and learn to accept all parts of themselves. In this acceptance, Fours no longer need to feel different or special because they are uniquely themselves, and they are also interconnected with others and the universe. They may even reach a place where they accept the past pain and suffering because it has made them who they are today. As Riso and Hudson write,

> Once liberated from their Basic Fear (of having no identity and no personal significance), Fours become a work of art and no longer need art as a substitute for the beauty that they find in abundance in themselves. Because they are

> aware of their Essential self and liberated from enmeshment
> with their emotional reactions, they can be more profoundly
> in touch with the ever-changing nature of reality and are
> inspired and delighted by it.[3]

The higher path of a Four can then lead to a deep knowing that their true Self is not a fixed self, but is ever changing and ever transforming throughout life, which is true for all the personality types. In this knowing, the Four can begin to live more open and present allowing themselves to be touched by the flow of experience on a moment-to-moment basis. The experience of opening to this flow allows a Four to open up to a deeper contact with others and the universe. At their core, Fours represent creation, the constant flow of manifestation, which is their gift to the other personality types by revealing that we all participate in the flow of divine creativity.

Another key to the development of a Four is being connected with the type's virtue of equanimity. Equanimity is about balance, and having an evenness of mental and emotional states. Balance is an embodiment involving having attention in the present, and being accepting of what is in that present moment.

In the Enneagram system as described by Helen Palmer, and other leading scholars in the field, equanimity is the highest expression for a Romantic. It is about finding balance in their lives which includes a balanced mind, balanced emotions and the ability to be in the present – not fondly longing for the past or anticipating the future, but being here now. This state of balance can bring an inner peace which runs so deep that outer circumstances, other people and events cannot tip the scales of balance. Emotions can be experienced and then released, and not drawn out into emotional dramas. Feelings and thoughts can drift like clouds across the sky with no attachment only observation. Energy is kept in the present moment giving us full awareness right now. Of course, this is the highest virtue for a Romantic, and there will be days when staying balanced is as hard to grasp as a slippery soap bubble.

One of my supervisors at a job complimented me on my capacity for equanimity. I had to smile because he even used that exact word without any knowledge of my interest in the Enneagram. It pertained to a difficult situation that I was in where I had to weigh all the information that I received, and then trust that there were certain elements that were out of my control. I also received some intuitive signs that my wishes would work out for the best. During that time, I didn't always feel that evenness of mind, and I did feel a lot of pressure from others to follow the status quo, but I knew that the decision was partly up to me, and I trusted that I would be guided to the right decision. It probably also helped that I am a Libra in the Zodiac system, and being balanced is one of my personal goals. When I have been way out of balance, I have felt agitated and on edge, and it seems that as I have become more conscious that I can't stay in that uncomfortable place for too long anymore. I need to address whatever is going on to re-gain my sense of balance. I do know that when I feel that state of equanimity that I feel blissful in a peaceful way – not escaping reality, but a sense of deep peace within. It can also be described as a deep, grounded awareness – not up in the mind, or in the fantasy world, but grounded in reality. Being in this state of equanimity seems to free up all kinds of energy to do what we feel most called to do in our lives. In this state of equanimity, there is an acceptance of what is happening in any given moment. Some moments are mundane, and others exhilarating, and if we can just be with whatever the moment brings, then we can enjoy it in its present form.

Fours have to look at how they judge, censor and criticize themselves because they don't match some ideal image. They need to see how these habits only distance themselves from their direct experience of life, and thus perpetuate a feeling of being disconnected, that leads to them abandoning their true Self. It is about learning how to accept themselves as they are, that means looking at the self-hate and the feeling states that they find negative. They need to learn that working through their emotional reactions and mental beliefs is only possible when they fully allow them. In terms of process, this means that a Four needs to not dramatize what she is feeling, and to not distance herself from the experience. It is meeting inner experience with equanimity, which involves allowing it, but not getting swept away by it. In this inner work, a Four can become more centered within, and less externally focused on relationships. The striving for the exciting and the dramatic can be replaced with a deep appreciation of peace and of simplicity. The need to be special can be replaced by an acceptance of being human, and connected to all of humankind.

As the layers are peeled away, the Four can be faced with a state of being lost, but instead of quickly filling this emptiness, the Four can fully experience it, and discover a place that feels free and peaceful within. As they go deeper into the emptiness, they can begin to find and discover their true Self, which was there all along. They can experience center and balance within, and no longer need to long for the Being that they felt separated from because they discover that they are that Being that they have been seeking all along.[4]

The healing journey of a Romantic can be a long winding path through one relationship after another, and creating one drama after another. The awareness begins when the individual looks within for the answers. No lover, friend or counselor can heal another person's lost connection with their Being. They can only act as guides in the search for Self. Ultimately, the healing for a Romantic will come from within which can lead to living a more conscious life, and making choices from a deeper place of knowing than reacting to the ever-changing winds of emotions. The knowing can come when they allow themselves to face the empty place within. It can be frightening to go there alone, but if they allow themselves to take that journey, they can discover their personal truth and their personal story which is theirs alone. People may accompany them on their life's journey, but they have to find their own way to discovering their whole Self which has been with them from the beginning.

Maitri writes about the healing journey of a Type Four,

She begins to find and recognize herself, to experience her original face before she was born, to paraphrase the Zen koan. A sense of connection arises, a sense of recognition of herself when all has been stripped away. She gradually begins to experience herself as a shining star in the firmament—a real star, rather than the imitation one she has tried to be. [5]

May all Romantics realize that they are shining stars, and allow their light to shine for the world to see.

Epilogue

Since writing this book, I have discovered some new insights into the roots of a Romantic. As I wrote in Chapter Two on *The Early Childhood of the Romantic*, I felt that the roots of a Romantic began in a child's personal experience of their parents. I still believe that is true for many Romantics, but recently in my counseling work, I have discovered that these roots could go further back than I realized.

Through past life regression work, and other tools such as dreamwork, I have personally discovered that the roots of my own Romantic go back to a previous lifetime. In this lifetime, the seeds of the Romantic were planted, and began to develop, and they continued to grow and flourish in my current lifetime. I haven't read anything on this particular subject, but, there could very well be other counselors who have discovered this fact when working with the Enneagram, and past life regression work. It is amazing to think that we may have been embodying our particular Enneagram type for many lifetimes. As we become more conscious, I feel that this insight will become more readily available for many of us who are on the path of conscious evolution.

I wish you many enlightening insights and revelations on your own personal journey of self-discovery, and I leave you with this quote:

There is one spectacle grander than the sea, that is the sky; there is one spectacle grander than the sky, that is the interior of the soul. Victor Hugo, Les Miserables (1862)

৵৽

Appendix A

The Nine Personality Types from www.enneagramworldwide.com

Type	Type Name	The Enneagram Type System
1	The Perfectionist	
2	The Giver	
3	The Performer	
4	The Romantic	
5	The Observer	
6	The Loyal Skeptic	
7	The Epicure	
8	The Protector	
9	The Mediator	

Appendix B

The Riso-Hudson Type Names and 18 Wing Subtype Names from their book *The Wisdom of the Enneagram* (New York: Bantam Books, 1999), pp. 11-12, 70

Type	Type Name	Wing	Subtype Names	The Eneagram Type System
1	The Reformer	9	The Idealist	
		2	The Advocate	
2	The Helper	1	The Servant	
		3	The Host/Hostess	
3	The Achiever	2	The Charmer	
		4	The Professional	
4	The Individualist	3	The Aristocrat	
		5	The Bohemian	
5	The Investigator	4	The Iconoclast	
		6	The Problem-Solver	
6	The Loyalist	5	The Defender	
		7	The Buddy	
7	The Enthusiast	6	The Entertainer	
		8	The Realist	
8	The Challenger	7	The Independent	
		9	The Bear	
9	The Peacemaker	8	The Referee	
		1	The Dreamer	

Appendix C

Riso & Hudson's Levels of Development for the Four from their book *The Wisdom of the Enneagram* (New York: Bantam Books, 1999), p. 188

	Level	Key Term	Levels of Development for the Type Four
H E A L T H Y	1	Life-Embracing Life-Enhancing	Fours let go of their belief that they are more flawed than others and are thus freed from self-absorption. Their Basic Desire, to find themselves and their significance, is also achieved and thus their problems with their identity and its stability are solved. They are self-renewing, redemptive, and revelatory.
	2	Introspective Sensitive	Fours focus on their own feelings and preferences to establish a clear sense of personal identity. Self-image: "I am sensitive, different and self-aware."
	3	Self-Revealing Creative	Fours reinforce their self-image by expressing their individuality through creative action. They are eloquent and subtle, exploring their feelings and impressions and finding ways of sharing with others. Their creativity is highly personal but often has universal implications.
A V E R A G E	4	Romanticizing Individualistic	Fours begin to fear that their changing feelings will not sustain them and their creativity, so they use their imaginations to prolong and intensify their moods. They use fantasy and style to bolster their individuality and begin to dream of someone who will rescue them.
	5	Self-Absorbed Temperamental	Fours worry that others will not recognize or appreciate them and their uniqueness, so they play hard to get – testing others to see if they are really interested in them. Aloof, self-conscious, and melancholy, they believe that their fragility will attract a rescuer and keep others away.
	6	Self-Indulgent Decadent	Fours fear that life's demands will force them to give up their dreams, and they despair that they will never be rescued. They feel they are missing out on life, and envy the stability of others, so they exempt themselves from "the rules," becoming sensual, pretentious, and unproductive.
U N H E A L T H Y	7	Hateful Alienated	Fours fear that they are wasting their lives, and this may be true. To save their self-image, they reject everyone and everything that does not support their view of themselves or their emotional demands. Their repressed rage results in depression, apathy and constant fatigue.
	8	Self-Rejecting Clinically Depressed	Fours have become so desperate to be the individual of their fantasies that they hate everything about themselves that does not correspond to it. They loathe themselves and hate others for failing to save them. They may sabotage whatever good is left in their lives.
	9	Despairing Life-Denying	The realization that they have wasted their lives pursuing futile fantasies is too much for unhealthy Fours. They may attempt to elicit rescue through self-destructive behavior or simply end their lives to escape their negative self-consciousness. In some cases, they may commit crimes of passion.

Appendix D

The Seven Greek Goddess Archetypes are the inner patterns that live within all of us, and that can consciously or unconsciously influence us at different points in our life. There are two excellent books that I recommend about these Greek Goddesses – *Goddesses in Every Woman* by Jean Shinoda Bolen, and *The Goddess Within* by Jennifer Barker Woolger and Roger J. Woolger. There is also a book about the Greek Gods entitled *Gods in Everyman* by Jean Shinoda Bolen.

Aphrodite, the Love Goddess focused on romance, relationship, sensual pleasures, beauty and fashion. She is also known as the goddess of painting, sculpture, architecture, poetry and music. A time of life focused on relationship and social activities.

Artemis, the Nature Goddess with a love of the outdoors known as adventurous, independent, and a loner following the beat of her own drum. She is close to animals, the hunt, and those cycles of nature that rule the animal as much as the human world. A moon goddess, she rules over all instinctual life, emphasizing the body rather than the head. A time of life focused on the outdoors, and achievement through sports and other physical challenges.

Athena, the Goddess of Justice, known as a strong, independent, career-minded woman who is ruled by her head rather than her heart. This goddess rules technology, science, practical crafts, literary arts, education, and intellectual life in all its forms. A time of achievement through career and possibly being a feminist.

Demeter, Mother Earth, a goddess focused on children, nurturing, cooking, gardening, and the home. Known as the Lady of the Plants, she has a deep connection to all aspects of food,

Donna M. Fisher-Jackson, M.A.

growth, cycles of the crops, harvesting and preserving. A time of life where the focus is on being a Mother, a Grandmother, and a Caretaker of Others.

Hera, the Goddess of Marriage, focused on status, social achievement, and can be known as the woman who stands behind her man. As the wife of the god Zeus, she rules over all kinds of partnerships and public roles where a woman has power, responsibility, or leadership. A time of achievement through partnership.

Hestia, the Goddess of the Hearth, embodies the patient and dependable woman who finds comfort in solitude, and has a sense of wholeness that comes from within. She is felt to be present in the living flame at the center of the home, temple and city. A more inward time of life focused on personal and/or spiritual growth.

Persephone, the Mystic and the Maiden Goddess is known for her intuitive abilities and interests in the metaphysical and spiritual sides of life. As Queen of the Dead, she rules over all aspects of contact with the underworld, the spirit world, or the realm of the departed. She is also concerned with mediumship, channeling, visionary skills, occult matters, and areas of psychic healing. A time of life that can be more introspective focused on delving into the unconscious and possibly the other side.

Suggested Reading

The following books in order by author are books that can give you more information on the Enneagram, on creativity, and on the healing journey:

Bolen, J. S. (1989). *Gods in everyman: A new psychology of men's lives and loves.* New York: Harper Perennial.

Bolen, J. S. (1984). *Goddesses in everywoman: A new psychology of women.* New York: Harper & Row.

Caldwell, C. (Ed.). (1997). *Getting in touch: The guide to new body-centered therapies.* Wheaton, IL: The Theosophical Publishing House.

Cameron, J. with Bryan, M. (1992). *The artist's way: A spiritual path to higher creativity.* New York: G. P. Putnam's Sons.

Cameron, J. (1996). *The vein of gold: A journey to your creative heart.* New York: G. P. Putnam's Sons.

Covington, S. & Beckett, L. (1988). *Leaving the enchanted forest: The path from relationship addiction to intimacy.* San Francisco: Harper.

Hendrix, H. (1988). *Getting the love you want: A guide for couples.* New York: Harper Perennial.

Herrera, H. (1983). *Frida: A biography of Frida Kahlo.* New York: HarperCollins.

Johnson, R. A. (1989). *He: Understanding masculine psychology.* New York: Harper Perennial.

Johnson, R. A. (1989). Sh*e: Understanding feminine psychology.* New York: Harper Perennial.

Johnson, R. A. (1983). *We: Understanding the psychology of romantic love.* San Francisco: Harper.

Linn, D. (1996). *The secret language of signs.* New York: Ballantine Books.

Donna M. Fisher-Jackson, M.A.

Maitri, S. (2005). *The enneagram of passions and virtues: Finding the way home.* New York: Jeremy P. Tarcher/Penquin.

Maitri, S. (2000). *The spiritual dimension of the enneagram: Nine faces of the soul.* New York: Penquin Putnam.

Naranjo, C. (1994). *Character and neurosis: An integrative view.* Nevada City, CA: Gateways/IDHHB.

Palmer, H. (1988). *The enneagram: Understanding yourself and the others in your life.* San Francisco: HarperCollins.

Palmer, H. (1995). *The enneagram in love & work: Understanding your intimate & business relationships.* San Francisco: HarperCollins.

Riley Fitch, N. (1993). *Anais: The erotic life of Anais Nin.* Boston: Little, Brown & Company.

Riso, D. R. with Hudson, R. (1996). *Personality types: Using the enneagram for self-discovery.* New York: Houghton Mifflin.

Riso, D. R. & Hudson, R. (1999). *The wisdom of the enneagram: The complete guide to psychological and spiritual growth for the nine personality types.* New York: Bantam Books.

Sanford, J. (1980). *The invisible partners: How the male and female in each of us affects our relationships.* New York: Paulist Press.

Scarf, M. (1987). *Intimate partners: patterns in love and marriage.* New York: Random House.

Zuercher, S. (2001). *Merton: An enneagram profile.* Nortre Dame: Ave Maria Press.

Zweig, C. (2003). *The holy longing: The hidden power of spiritual yearning.* New York: Jeremy P. Tarcher/Putnam.

Zweig, C. and Wolf, S. (1997). *Romancing the shadow: A guide to soul work for a vital, authentic life.* New York: Ballantine Wellspring.

Notes

Introduction

1. Riso, D. R. & Hudson, R., *The Wisdom of the Enneagram: The complete guide to psychological and spiritual growth for the nine personality types* (New York: Bantam, 1999), pp. 19-22.

2. Ibid., pp. 22-24.

3. Palmer, *The Enneagram*, p. 4.

4. Riso & Hudson, *The Wisdom of the Enneagram*, p. 24.

5. Maitri, S., *The Spiritual Dimension of the Enneagram: Nine faces of the soul* (New York: Penquin Putnam, 2000), p. 13.

6. Palmer, *The Enneagram* p. 168.

Chapter 1: The Mystery of the Romantic

1. Palmer, *The Enneagram*, pp. 171-172.

2. Riso & Hudson, *The Wisdom of the Enneagram*, p. 180.

3. Maitri, *The Spiritual Dimension of the Enneagram*, p. 133.

4. Ibid., p. 138.

5. Riso & Hudson, *The Wisdom of the Enneagram*, pp. 183-184

6. Ibid., p. 184.

7. *Webster's Ninth New Collegiate Dictionary* (Springfield, MA: Merriam-Webster, 1983), p. 703

Chapter 2: The Early Childhood of the Romantic

1. Maitri, *The Spiritual Dimension of the Enneagram*, p. 138

2. Ibid., p. 138.

3. Love, P. & Shulkin, S., *Imago theory and the psychology of attraction* in Family Journal; Alexandria; July 2001

4. Hendrix, H., *Getting the Love You Want: A guide for couples* (New York: HarperPerennial, 1988), p. 37

Chapter 3: The Romantic in Relationships

1. Maitri, *The Spiritual Dimension of the Enneagram*, pp. 133-134.

Donna M. Fisher-Jackson, M.A.

2. Maitri, S., *The Enneagram of Passions and Virtues: Finding your way home* (New York: Jeremy P. Tarcher/Penquin, 2005), p. 18.

3. Palmer, *The Enneagram*, p. 183.

4. Riso & Hudson, *The Wisdom of the Enneagram*, p. 71

5. Zweig, C. & Wolf, S., *Romancing the Shadow: A guide to soul work for a vital, authentic life* (New York: Ballentine Wellspring, 1997), p. 145.

6. Scarf, M. *Intimate Partners: Patterns in love and marriage* (New York: Random House, 1987), p. 14

7. Sanford, J., *The Invisible Partners: How the male and female in each of us affects our relationships* (New York: Paulist Press, 1980), p. 19

8. Palmer, H., *The Enneagram in Love and Work: Understanding your intimate and business relationships* (San Francisco: HarperCollins, 1995), p. 120

9. Johnson, R. A., *She: Understanding feminine psychology* (New York: HarperPerennial, 1989), p. 3

10. Tuch, R., *The Single Woman- Married Man Syndrome* (Northvale, NJ: Jason Aronson, 2000), p. 30.

11. Scarf, M., *Intimate Partners*, pp. 18-22.

12. Ibid., p. 141.

13. Ibid., p. 132.

14. Whitmont, E.C., *The Symbolic Quest: Basic concepts of analytical psychology* (Princeton, NJ: Princeton University Press, 1969), pp. 179-180.

15. Sanford, J., *The Invisible Partners*, p. 85.

Chapter 4: The Discovery of Self

1. Riso & Hudson, *The Wisdom of the Enneagram*, pp. 54-55.

2. Zweig, C., *The Holy Longing: The hidden power of spiritual yearning* (New York: Jeremy P. Tarcher/Putnam, 2003), p. 71

3. Maitri, *The Spiritual Dimension of the Enneagram*, pp. 140-141.

4. Riso & Hudson, *The Wisdom of the Enneagram*, p. 193.

5. Naranjo, C., *Character and neurosis: An integrative view*, (Nevada City, CA: Gateways/IDHHB, 1994)

6. Maitri, *The Spiritual Dimension of the Enneagram*, p. 146.

7. Ibid., p. 147.

8. Ibid., pp. 147-148.

9. Riso & Hudson, *The Wisdom of the Enneagram*, pp. 75-76.

10. Riso, D. R. with Hudson, R., *Personality Types: Using the enneagram for self-discovery*, (New York: Houghton Mifflin, 1996), pp. 136-138.

Chapter 5: The Creative Path of the Romantic

1. Riso with Hudson, *Personality Types*, p. 136.

2. *Frida Kahlo Postcards*, (San Francisco: Chronicle Book, 1991), Introduction

Chapter 6: The Healing Path through Relationships

1. Sanford, *The Invisible Partners*, p. 13.

2. Ibid., p. 14.

3. Ibid., p. 15.

4. Ibid., p. 15.

5. Ibid., p. 60.

6. Jung, C.G., *The Archetypes of the Collective Unconscious: Collected works 9, 1*, (New York: Pantheon Books, 1959), p. 29.

7. Sanford, *The Invisible Partners*, p. 72.

8. Ibid., p. 112.

9. Johnson, *She*, p. 62.

10. Ibid., p. 69.

Chapter 7: The Healing Path through Addictions

1. Covington, S. & Beckett, L., *Leaving the Enchanted Forest: The path from relationship addiction to intimacy*, (San Francisco: HarperSanFrancisco, 1988), p. xvi

2. Ibid., p. 11.

3. Zweig, *The Holy Longing*, p. 170.

4. Ibid., p. 173.

Chapter 8: The Healing Path through Spirituality

1. Zweig, *The Holy Longing*, pp. 70-71.

Donna M. Fisher-Jackson, M.A.

2. Zuercher, S., *Merton: An enneagram profile*, (Notre Dame: Ave Maria Press, 2001), p. 139.

Chapter 9: The Four Elements of Healing: Water, Earth, Fire and Air
1. *Webster's Ninth New Collegiate Dictionary*, p. 660.
2. Brown, D., *The DaVinci Code*, (New York: Doubleday, 2003), p. 203.
3. Ibid., p. 203.
4. Ibid., p. 204.
5. Bolen, J.S., *Goddesses in Everywoman: A new psychology of women*, (New York: Harper & Row, 1984), pp. 239, 256
6. Zweig & Wolf, *Romancing the Shadow*, p. 206.
7. Ibid., p. 206.
8. Ibid., p. 210.
9. Dream group guidelines from Greg Bogart, Ph.D., MFT, a psychotherapist and astrologer, in the San Francisco Bay area of CA.

Chapter 10: The Conscious Evolution of the Four
1. Riso & Hudson, *The Wisdom of the Enneagram*, p. 93.
2. Ibid., p. 202.
3. Ibid., p. 204
4. Maitri, *The Spiritual Dimension of the Enneagram*, pp. 152-154.
5. Ibid., p. 154.

The Next Book by Donna M. Fisher-Jackson, M.A.

Clara & Irving

A Past Life Love Story

Based on the True Story of a Romantic

Clara and Irving's love story began in the Roaring Twenties in a seacoast village called Onset, an Indian name which means *The Sandy Landing Place* on Cape Cod, Massachusetts. In its heyday, Onset was known as a summer retreat and many tourists from the surrounding states came to enjoy its amusements which included beaches, casinos, vaudeville theatres, and dance halls. Onset also hosted a Spiritualist summer camp in its early days similar to Lilydale, New York.

Onset was the beginning of Clara and Irving's love story....one that lasted longer than both would ever imagine....from one lifetime to the next. In Romantic fashion, their love began in a 1920's vaudeville theatre, and the theatre became a stage for their love affair in years later.

To find out when this next book is being published, sign up for Donna's newsletter, *Iris Insights*, at www.DonnaFisherJackson.com.

Made in the USA